The Beauty of Reiki

Reiki I: Self Healing

Patty Tahara Rassouli

ISBN - 13:978-0692912935

Introduction

Life is complicated. Many of us believe that.

Life is stressful. A whole lot of people would say that is 100% true.

I believe:

> "Life can be simpler.
>
> Life can be mostly peaceful."

These two sentences can become true if we learn Reiki, universal healing energy. It is not just the knowledge of Reiki and how it works, but the Reiki philosophy and the importance of meditation. We also learn the value of a strong daily routine to create regular good habits that promote and maintain good mental and physical heath.

For myself, learning and experiencing Reiki has been the single most important "thing" that I have ever learned. No fact, subject, or knowledge in school can compare to my experience of living a Reiki life. It has changed who I am, my relationships, my ideas, everything.

I learned Reiki in 2009 by chance, although I would have to say today that there is no such thing as chance. I went to my usual Sunday yoga class at Dancing Shiva in West Hollywood to take my teacher, Mas Vidal's class. He was away and Tuesday May Thomas substituted. She was a Reiki Master and told us about a Reiki class she was giving in two weeks; coincidentally, I had picked up a book about Reiki at the library just days before. That book had caught my attention because it was just lying by itself on the shelf away from all the other upright books as if calling out to me. I devoured that book in one sitting, fascinated by what I was learning so that when Tuesday mentioned her upcoming class, I signed up immediately because this was one class I was not going to miss.

Through a meditation, Tuesday attuned me to the Reiki energy. I can't really say that I immediately felt the energy coursing through me. What happened was that I did self-Reiki every day as I continue to do. The energy slowly cleared up imbalances and insecurities that I had been carrying around since childhood. It was and is a gradual, steady process. Over time, I felt more sure of myself and more joyous. I wanted to share this energy with everyone, so they could experience this same wonderful feeling. In fact, I was so passionate about promoting Reiki with my loved ones that some of them became put off by my enthusiasm. It was as if they were thinking, "Oh, oh, here comes Patty with the Reiki." It took me a while to learn how to temper my excitement and to allow people to ask for Reiki rather than my constantly offering it.

What I want to emphasize is that we as humans are always going to be in and out of balance because lifestyle, events and people can toss us around like a roller coaster, elevating us to new heights only to sometimes send us plummeting down. Therefore, even though Reiki can get us clear, it's not that we remain always balanced. It's a continual practice of self-care, Reiki and meditation which can all help us to get back on track whenever we unwittingly take a detour or go the wrong way.

Over the years, my main mission has been to teach Reiki. It is so easy to learn and is accessible to everyone, even children. I have great respect for all healing arts but the beauty of Reiki is that it doesn't require years of study. You can begin at once, and you can see small results almost immediately. You will feel calmer and more relaxed. Moreover, if you continue, life becomes clearer as you set aside unhelpful mental patterns and learn to be your best self.

Table of Contents

Chapter One:
Everything About Reiki ……………………………………………………………6

Chapter Two:
The Reiki Meditation……………………………………………………………..17

Chapter Three:
The Value of Meditation………………………………………………………36

Chapter Four:
The Chakras………………………………………………………………………..47

Chapter Five:
Understanding Ourselves………………………………………………………63

Chapter Six:
The Daily Routine…………………………………………………………………75

Chapter Seven:
Relationships, The Animal Kind, Too………………………………………..86

Last Words………………………………………………………………………….97

CHAPTER ONE:
Everything About Reiki

What is Reiki?

Reiki is the placing of hands on or above a person's body, allowing universal energy to enter a person, to remove blockages and to help heal. The life force in our bodies called ki (other names: qi, chi, prana, etc.) must flow effortlessly for good health. When ki is blocked, then harmful thinking patterns, emotional duress and eventually illness can occur. Reiki helps to keep our life force flowing.

Typical Reiki Session

A typical Reiki session begins with the client lying face up. If lying down is not possible, a sitting position is also fine. The client is fully clothed but should remove shoes, a watch, and other accessories. The Reiki practitioner puts slightly cupped hands over certain positions on the body. Sometimes the practitioner touches the body and sometimes she places hands above the body. A session can range from about 30 minutes to more than an hour, depending on the client's needs and the experience of the practitioner.

There are eight basic positions on the front of the body and four more positions on the back. Usually each position is held from about three - five minutes. Depending on the client's specific concerns, it may be necessary to remain on certain positions for longer periods of time or to treat other parts of the body, such as arms, hands, elbows, knees, etc. Sometimes, a person will need to be comforted so placing the hands in a cupping position over the chin will be necessary. The feet are often the last position in order to ground the client.

After a session, the client is usually calm and relaxed. Then the healing can begin.

How Does Reiki Work?

When a person is stressed out, he goes for the fast food, the alcohol, the sleeping pills, the drugs, the unhealthy sex, excess shopping, mindless TV and technology usage, etc. to numb the pain. These actions further bind a person to an unhealthy lifestyle.

If a person is totally relaxed, then she can do the good things that she needs to do for optimum health. For example, after a Reiki session, a person may feel calm and centered. On the way home from the Reiki session, he might feel like cooking a simple healthy meal instead of picking up fast food. After eating well, a walk may seem like a good idea. The next morning instead of downing endless cups of coffee and doughnuts, this person may opt for a cup of coffee and whole-grain cereal and fruit. This is the way Reiki works—a person starts to feel better, and then all the healthy and beneficial things to do are much more possible.

As a person starts to implement better choices, this in turn promotes more healthy behavior. This is the manner in which Reiki works, clearing the individual so she feels well, and then it is always up to the person's free will to implement the good choices and behavior.

Reiki can put an individual on the right path, taking him to the gate of healing. However, it is always up to the person how she enters the gate, how hard he wants to work and how far she wishes to go. Healing is always left up to the individual.

Important Concept of Reiki

In fact, some people may think that Reiki is not working because they see themselves making the choices and doing the hard work. Of course, they are the ones buying the healthy produce and making the smoothies. They make the decision to join an exercise class or submit their resume for a new job or decide to watch less TV. What they don't realize is that Reiki started the process, getting them relaxed and clear so that they could arrive at that important mindset.

One Client's Experience

This person was very depressed. He came in walking slowly, showing little expression in his face. He even talked softly in a monotone. After the session, he felt calmer and smiled as he left. After two weeks, he had, with his doctor's approval, decreased his depression medication dosage. This was very significant because it reduced some nagging side effects. Did he believe that Reiki had anything to do with it? No, because it was his decision to contact his doctor and ask if the medication could be decreased. However, what he forgot was how desperate he felt before the session and how immediately after, how much calmer he was. Reiki helped to clear him, and he was able to make better decisions. This person did not continue with Reiki because he did not recognize that Reiki was working. He attributed everything to himself which was, in fact, true. He had been the one to call the doctor. However, how long had he been in that state of depression before he tried Reiki? Almost a year. Reiki got him to that place where he was able to make that call.

A Student's Experience

Prior to taking the Reiki I class, this student, who has a very demanding business, knew she had to do something to manage the constant stress. She started to pay attention to her diet and knew she needed some type of exercise, so she signed up at a yoga studio, purchasing a pack of classes. However, weeks passed, and she just couldn't get the motivation to go. However, after the Reiki I class, she suddenly felt like going to the studio. From that point on, she found the enthusiasm to practice yoga and also to develop her own self practice. Reiki got her to the frame of mind so she could help herself. Today this student does a variety of healing modalities to manage her very busy and challenging life.

How Do You Learn Reiki?

After having good experiences with Reiki, some people choose to learn it so that they can self-Reiki whenever they wish to maintain their own well-being and also to help their family and friends.

A Reiki Master Teacher guides a student into a meditation. At that time, the Reiki Master Teacher places the Reiki system into the person's hands and crown chakra. This meditation takes a very short time and when it is done, a student will be able to access the healing energy through his own hands. Once a person is "attuned" to the energy, she always has the ability to do Reiki even if she stops practicing for years.

The more a person accesses Reiki, the stronger the energy becomes. If a person can live as cleanly as possible without anger and with great compassion, the energy will flourish.

Is Reiki Working?

The best way to measure the benefits of Reiki is to measure it over time. Because Reiki is a subtle energy, it is easier to assess when it is seen through time markers such as one month, three months, six months, one year, three years, and so forth. Ask yourself questions such as:

How am I different?

What am I now doing that I didn't used to do?

What am I not doing that I used to do?

Have any of my beliefs changed?

How are my emotions?

How is my mood?

It is very helpful to keep a journal and in this way, a person can clearly see the changes that have occurred.

What is Reiki's Origin?

Mikao Usui

The healing art of Reiki is attributed to Mikao Usui, a man who was born in Japan in 1865. It is often said that Usui rediscovered Reiki, that it may have existed since the beginning of time.

Usui, who was seeking spiritual knowledge, made a pilgrimage to Mt. Kurama near Kyoto, Japan in the 1920s. There he fasted and meditated with the intention of enlightenment. On the 21st day, while Usui was meditating, the Reiki system became known to him. As he came down the mountain, he hurt his foot. He immediately put his hands over the injury and his foot became better.

What Usui found so remarkable about Reiki healing was that he could administer this energy healing without feeling depleted as some energy work can be very draining.

(For example, many of my students have been massage therapists. They have mentioned, how sometimes, after a day's work or after a particular client, they feel emotionally and physically drained. This situation almost never happens with Reiki because the practitioner is not using her own energy; she uses universal energy. There are also protective procedures one can do before and after a session to further ensure that one isn't affected by a client's negative energy.)

Usui treated many people who became well as a result of Reiki. However, he found that the same people that he had helped would later come back because their various ailments and diseases had returned. Usui thought it would be better to teach people how to do Reiki so that they could help themselves. As a result, Usui devised a teaching methodology which is the foundation for teaching Reiki today.

Chujiro Hayashi

A very important person whom Usui taught was Chujiro Hayashi, a medical doctor and former Naval officer. Hayashi set up a Reiki clinic in Tokyo called Hayashi Reiki Keakyu-kai which had eight beds and 16 practitioners. Two practitioners worked on one client at a time.

While Usui worked mainly on the head and specifically on the physical location of the presenting problem, Hayashi devised other positions on the body. The positions we use today are mostly influenced by Hayashi.

Hawayo Takata

Reiki came to the West via Hawayo Takata, an American born to Japanese immigrants. Takata lived in Hawaii where she married and had children. Her husband died in his 30s and Takata had many stresses and difficulties taking care of her family.

In the 1930s, Takata traveled to Japan to tell her family about her sister's death and to try to get help for her many ailments—stomach and lung problems. By chance she met Chujiro Hayashi's daughter who told her about her father's Reiki clinic. Takata became a patient and after regular treatments for several months, she was cured. As a result, she asked Hayashi to train her in Reiki and to help her set up a Reiki practice in Hawaii which he did.

When Mrs. Takata taught, she charged very high fees to ensure that Reiki would be respected and honored. She also would never let students write down the symbols that are used in Reiki. That is why there are some variations of the more complicated symbols.

Although the symbols can now be found in books and on the internet, I follow the traditional teaching of only showing the symbols to the students in person. I also ask that they refrain from showing the symbols to people who are not attuned to the energy.

The Levels of Reiki

Reiki is divided into four levels, Reiki I, Reiki II, Reiki III and Reiki Master Teacher. Some studies of Reiki combine Reiki III with the Master Teacher level.

Reiki I

Students learn the system of Reiki and its history. In addition, students learn how a person can self-heal by laying his hands on the Reiki body positions. Reiki I is about self-study, reflecting on one's habits and family patterns. In addition, the importance of a meditation practice is emphasized, and students learn the Reiki Meditation and work on its five principles. They also learn about the chakras and how they influence our physical, mental and emotional well-being.

Students are encouraged to begin a routine of self-care which includes not only Reiki and meditation, but regular exercise, nutritious food and good thoughts.

Students should stay in Reiki I for a minimum of at least two to three months before moving on to Reiki II. Some people, however, will feel satisfied in Reiki I and are happy to remain there. Others will want to study Reiki II. It is recommended that students take the time to absorb the energy and only go on to Reiki II when they strongly feel the need to do so. Sometimes if students move too quickly among the levels, the energy is too overwhelming, and they feel ungrounded, not really understanding why. These people inevitably leave Reiki.

Reiki II

Reiki II is the practitioner level, and it is often the most life changing. Students continue self-healing, but now they are able to address emotional and mental issues. Furthermore, students will have stronger Reiki energy and may want to help others professionally.

Students learn to send Reiki long distance: This is an extremely helpful tool as loved ones and people in need might live across town, in another city, or even on another continent.

In Reiki II, students develop an even more focused daily routine with more emphasis on meditation and the beginning of doing service for others.

It is recommended that students remain in Reiki II for at least one year, and students should be cautioned it is at this level where their most important issues come up and must be addressed. They must not fear this challenge as they will be able to handle it, emerging from this year of growth and enlightenment with immeasurable gains and benefits.

Reiki III

Level III is all about living a lifestyle conducive to Reiki, following a life of the five Reiki principles. It is a major commitment and must be honored. Students will be encouraged to have a deep meditation practice, to adopt a grounding activity/exercise such as tai chi, yoga, gardening, jogging, martial arts, etc., to follow a healthy and clean diet free of processed chemicals and preservatives, and to create a mind that thinks good thoughts. At this time, the importance of service takes on a very major role, and Level III people understand that they cannot look away when others are in need. It is their responsibility to help others when they cross their path.

Reiki III is a joyous level and level III practitioners have the same ability to do Reiki as a Reiki Master Teacher. The only difference is that they do not teach and pass on the ability to access energy; therefore, some people who have no desire for teaching, will stay at this level.

I always encourage students to learn how to teach Reiki because even though they may not want to teach it formally, they can still pass attunements for the close people in their lives. For example, perhaps, a loved one is transitioning—a Reiki attunement can be very calming, very comforting for the person. Also, students will always have the option to teach it, should they ever change their mind.

Students should be aware that advanced Reiki degrees may speed up karma.

Reiki Master Teacher

A Reiki Master Teacher instructs all levels of Reiki and passes Reiki energy to students, giving them the ability to draw the Reiki energy in to help themselves and others. A Reiki Master Teacher will always be learning as the experiences in Reiki will reveal valuable lessons not found in Reiki books.

The Master Teacher is committed to a lifestyle of sharing Reiki and offering service within and outside of Reiki. When people are in need, the Master Teacher must try his best to help. She cannot ignore others' needs no matter how inconvenient or difficult. A Master Teacher upholds honor and integrity, living with the intent of having a meaningful and authentic life.

A Reiki Master Teacher is also committed to spreading the word about Reiki and teaching it to as many people as possible to share this helpful and wonderful knowledge. Reiki helps people, families, communities, societies and ultimately the world to live at their full potential with understanding and compassion.

Imagine if the whole world practiced this kind energy. Perhaps, this idea is not too far-fetched as more and more people are hearing about it. If you recall, yoga in the 1960s was viewed as something that "hippies" did, and now it is mainstream, prescribed by doctors.

Reiki Hand Positions

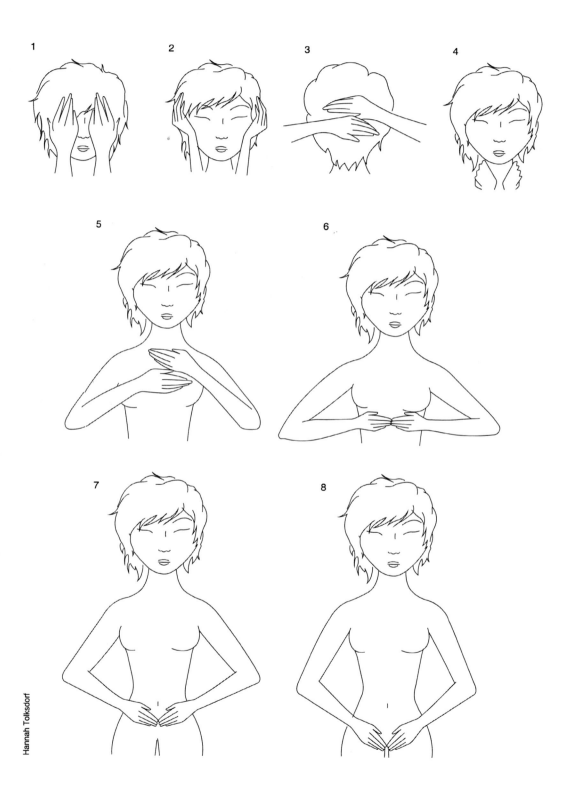

Hannah Tolksdorf

Reiki Hand Positions

Over the face
Blocks out the world. Promotes a feeling of peace and calm. Works on the third eye, intuition. If one is confused, this position aids clarity.

On the temples
Balances and calms the brain for better focus and clearer thinking. Good for effective decision-making.

Back of the head
Balances the body systems—nervous, endocrine—to help hormones, brain and body systems to work well. As a result, a better mood and sense of well-being.

Over the throat
Enables us to see and speak our truths; thus, understanding ourselves more honestly for a more effective life. Enhances communication skills and the ability to speak up.

The heart
Soothes the heart's emotions. Helps one to be more receptive and open to others and new situations. Forgiveness and compassion are possible, all of which create better health.

The solar plexus
Increases one's will and determination for strong identity. Sense of self is strengthened as well as confidence.

Under navel
Genitals
Clears old emotional wounds. Works on relationships. The seat of creativity and healthy sexuality.

Perineum/
rectum
Fears and anxiety are lessened as a person feels more grounded. Less insecurity helps one to live more honestly, more authentically and more emotionally balanced.

Other Positions (Not Shown)

Upper shoulders
Helps with burdens. Relieves held tension.

Back of heart
Works on heart and lungs. Helpful for grief.

Middle back
Eases guilt. Works on solar plexus.

Lower back
Releases tension from being burnt out mentally and/or physically. Can be caused by financial stress.

CHAPTER TWO:
The Reiki Meditation

Mikao Usui created The Reiki Meditation, five principles universal in their importance. It's helpful to reflect upon these principles daily, so that we can live each day to its utmost and to our own potential. The words "Just for today" are very very important because they place emphasis that good living is created step by step in each and every moment.

Reiki Meditation:

Just for today, do not anger.

Just for today, do not worry.

Just for today, do your work honestly.

Just for today, have compassion for everyone and every situation.

Just for today, practice gratitude.

You can take time to say the Reiki principles before or after your regular meditation, or you can take thoughtful breaks throughout the day to reflect upon them. For example, as you get into your car to go to school or work, you can think about how fortunate you are to have transportation and a job or an opportunity to study. As you see a handicapped or elderly person making her way across the street, you may be reminded to be compassionate and also to be grateful for your own health. When a worrisome thought invades your mind, think about being in the present and how everything is fine at this moment. In this way, you can approach your life mindfully and with appreciation.

The five Reiki principles are not new ideas. What's important is that they are meditated upon daily to keep you present in the moment. Intention is a major part of Reiki philosophy, that we intend to abide by these sacred tenets and that we intend to create healthy lives for ourselves, our families, our friends and even our communities.

Anger

When we feel anger, it is because we have a different expectation of a person's reaction or how a situation should be. We have to acknowledge that just because we expected a certain result does not mean that it is necessarily the "right one." As we know, we humans are as diverse in as many ways as there are grains of sand on this earth. There is no one way to be human.

Sometimes our anger is justified. What we need to realize is at that time, that was the best that that person was capable of doing. People will say no, that person can do better, that person has actually done better.

Yes, that person can and probably has done better, but **AT THAT MOMENT**, that was her absolute best.

The Law of Being Human

We are all fallible and our lives are riddled with mistakes and regrets. The basic "Law of Being Human" means that even though we know the correct way to conduct ourselves, we don't always do it for a multitude of reasons. We feel crabby that day, an emotion of jealousy, spitefulness, competitiveness, stubbornness, insecurity, whatever, takes over and we don't behave properly. Maybe we were just hungry and became impatient. Perhaps we had a headache. Maybe we just didn't think. It can be so simple and so ordinary.

If we can understand this "law," then we can better accept a person/situation and not feel as angry. Of course, if a person is always hurting us, then it is best to remove ourselves from that person's company. That's just common sense, but for our trusted circle of family and friends, we can understand that they had a moment of being human as we all have and always will; therefore, everyone is deserving of forgiveness.

Letting Anger Go

When your emotions have settled down, it's up to you to have a discussion. More often than not, it is just a misunderstanding that a dialogue will clear up. If it isn't a misunderstanding, then you can state your thoughts and feelings, and it's up to the other person to accept them. It doesn't matter if she does or he doesn't. You will have released those emotions and they will no longer be lingering in your mind and body. Too many people are uncomfortable with the word confront. It doesn't have to be a battle. It can be as simple as a few words or a discussion.

Many people, not wanting a "confrontation," think that they can control their anger and take care of it themselves. These individuals lack the courage to address the person or the situation. By fearing discomfort or vulnerability, these people live a life of no resolution. They do not realize that by speaking about their anger to the person, the magnitude of it is immediately diminished. It also opens up the opportunity for better connections and intimacy. Yes, we can be closer with those whom we have undergone conflict with as it is a sharing in vulnerability. If we never go to that uncomfortable place of taking the step to address the person and/or the problem, we will not progress as a human being. Every situation is an opportunity to learn something about others and ourselves. Many times we will find out it was a misunderstanding or a difference in interpretation.

Why Anger Must Be Resolved

Anger that is not resolved turns into deep resentment. Louise Hay, the late author of *You Can Heal Your Life* and a huge proponent of the emotional connection to disease believed that cancer is rooted in deep resentment. What is resentment but anger that has not been released?

Harboring bad emotions in the body only makes them fester and grow larger than they deserve to be. One day, those suppressed but constantly simmering negative feelings may spiral out of control into cancer cells or a heart condition or some other severe pain in the body.

Sometimes you see people who are so angry that they will cut the offending person from their lives. Years will go by and these people will think that they are rid of that person when ironically, their connection is even stronger because it is unresolved. They can never forget that person and often the importance of that person grows disproportionately to the actual situation. It is healthier to address the person, try for a resolution, and then release it. Even if the problem is not resolved, those negative feelings will be released from your body. Only then can that person be relegated to the distant background of your life.

Express your anger in a healthy way to the person.

Release the anger from your mind/body.

Understand that you may not get a resolution, but that it is okay as you have done your part responsibly.

In the end, we are all human, thus fallible.

Forgive.

Worry

When you worry, your body tenses up, you breathe shallowly, and your overall sense of well-being is reduced. You have more chances to make mistakes, to get sick and to have injuries. In addition, you are depleting your body of healing oxygen. When you breathe from the tops of your lungs, less oxygen enters your body which means less nutrients are making their way to your organs, your skin, your bones, your teeth and hair, your cells and tissues. Worried people are not only less healthy, they are less beautiful!

What do you do when you are worrying?

First, understand that it is usually a projected worry for a person or situation in the future.

Bring yourself immediately to the present.

Observe your current situation.

If everything is fine, then acknowledge it and be grateful.

If everything is not fine, then look at what is not and how much is within your control.

Take care of your responsibility.

After that, just release as you have done your part.

Perspiration Helps

It is also very helpful to do something physical which causes you to perspire to counteract a worrisome feeling. Jogging, swimming, all sports, mopping the floor, washing the car, raking the leaves, etc. are all great. By doing this activity, it will take you out of that mental place just by the action itself and the perspiration is a release. However, you may have to push yourself to get started.

Life Acceptance

Practice life acceptance. If we can understand that all events and situations in life have value, then we can roll through the bad times, not letting the effects bother us too much. For example, let's imagine a close loved one dies unexpectedly. If we can find life acceptance, then we can look at our relationship and recognize how grateful we are for having known this person. It will further teach us the fragility of life, and we will learn to respect life even more, taking care to appreciate the special people in our lives now. It will bring us to the present, and we will benefit from this great sadness in our lives. We will be better.

What if we had negligent and hateful parents? Life acceptance teaches us to accept this tragic and sad reality. By accepting it, we can then move on, taking pleasure in creating our own healthy family and relationships. There is value in that pain as we understand how necessary it is to change that terrible pattern, creating a new life of love and warmth which we will treasure even more because we have the eternal contrast of that terrible life experience.

Imagine our loved one rejects us. How can life acceptance help us? We can look at the relationship through unprejudiced eyes and perhaps we will see and understand our role in the breakup. We are as flawed as our loved one; therefore, we contributed equally to the demise of our relationship. No one is totally blameless. We can accept that we have learned from this experience and that we will bring more comprehension to our next relationship. We are grateful for learning and know that our next relationship will be better because we are better.

Life acceptance also helps in all situations where we have no control. We accept and learn to live a life of faith, believing that we are on our journeys to learn, to expand, and to gain knowledge and wisdom. There is really no place for worry if we possess life acceptance.

New Ways of Thinking

After life acceptance, practice new ways of viewing situations, looking for other possibilities.

Imagine you got fired from a job that you had for several years. Of course, you would be sad and possibly angry and/or fearful for your loss. If you could accept this situation and look beyond the loss of position and financial gain, then you might see how you had become too complacent and even bored at times just going through the motions. Perhaps you stayed where you were because it was safe and easy. This loss may propel you in a completely different direction, one in which you become fully engaged and challenged.

What if you are involved in a lawsuit, and the mere fact of being sued and all the time and paperwork just seems so overwhelming? You could get very angry or fearful and look at your opponent with hate and disgust, or you can choose to look more neutrally at the situation. Perhaps there's something in all the chaos that you can learn from, that you can use productively in your life. You might learn to pay more attention to people, to see exactly who they are. You may change your attitude towards money and see that the stress of the possibility of paying money is really not as upsetting as it seems.

By changing your attitude, by looking at every negative situation in a different way, you can see that everything is for you, everything is for your learning, for your betterment. You might just express gratitude instead.

Believe that whatever happens is nudging you (if you are receptive to looking) towards something better and more beneficial. If you look at people's lives, their great successes, their new healthy relationships, their completely different direction in life, mostly all came when people were totally down, devastated and/or heartbroken.

Rumi, the 13th century poet wrote:

> **This being human is a guest house. Each morning is a new arrival. A joy, a depression, a meanness, some momentary awareness comes as an unexpected visitor…welcome and entertain them all. Treat each guest honorably. The dark thought, the shame, the malice, meet them at the door laughing and invite them in. Be grateful for whoever comes because each has been sent as a guide from beyond.**

According to Rumi, everything is to be welcomed because everything that comes your way has a purpose in your life. It's not happenstance. If you can believe this way of thinking, then living life is comfortable because you know that you are enough and that whatever comes your way, you will be able to handle it, to learn from it, and possibly to even enjoy it.

Or you can live a life…

of constant struggle,

of constant complaint,

of constant worry,

of constant anger,

of constant frustration.

The choice is all yours.

Compassion

We learn that we are all connected on this earth. When we hurt another, we hurt ourselves. Every living thing has a link to another, and we are all the same. As humans, some of us are funny, some of us are tall, some of us are musical, some of us are athletic, and the list goes on. What we all share is the human experience and the fact that we will live on this earth for "X" amount of years and then we will die. It is for this reason that we must be compassionate toward each other because we all undergo life's joys and tribulations. We are all the same.

On the front gate of the United Nations building, there is a poem written in Farsi by the 13th century Persian poet, Sa'adi who stressed humanity and our need for unity. Here is one translation for this poem but there are several others and some rhyming ones as well.

The sons of Adam are limbs of each other,
Having been created of one essence.
When the calamity of time affects one limb,
The other limbs cannot remain at rest.
If thou hast no sympathy for the troubles of others,
Thou art unworthy to be called by the name of Human.

Be Kind To Yourself First

Actually, a major problem is that many of us lack true compassion for ourselves. Too many of us berate ourselves daily by saying that we are not good enough, not capable enough, not beautiful enough, etc. How can we be compassionate towards others if we can barely stomach ourselves?

We must be kind, patient and tolerant towards ourselves first before we can even begin to be compassionate to others. It's hard to grasp the meaning that we are enough. But we are. Accept that there will always be someone smarter, richer, more talented, more beautiful, more athletic, but no person will have your unique combination of characteristics and abilities. If you find that you regard yourself harshly, remember to say and repeat the wonderful things about yourself. To make a new habit, it takes time, lots of repetition and daily work.

Compassionate Exercise

On a daily basis, how many times a day do you think/say something good about yourself?

_____0   _____1 - 5   _____ 6 - 10   _____ more than 10

On a daily basis, how many times a day do you think/say something good about others?

_____0   _____1 - 5   _____6 - 10   _____ more than 10

What are the three most special things about yourself?

1. _____

2. _____

3. _____

What are the three most special things about the closest person in your life?

1. _____

2. _____

3. _____

Do Your Work Honestly

Usui meant that we must practice meditation when he said for us to do our work honestly; however, most of us have to do other work in order to survive. In an ideal situation, you are doing work which you enjoy and are passionate about. When that occurs, your work will be of the purest and highest quality.

Many of us have yet to make that transition of feeling joyous about the work we do. In the meantime, we are at jobs, doing what we have to do. No matter how we may feel about these jobs, we can always pledge to do our best with the highest intention. Whatever our duties are, we should do them with appreciation and 100% of our effort. We may find that a formerly intolerable job situation becomes more agreeable. Furthermore, when we do things with integrity, a strong energy is created that benefits us by creating a better atmosphere and mental attitude. From that, anything wonderful can develop.

Gossip is Destructive

Doing your work honestly also means not partaking in gossip in the workplace. This is very difficult to do because if you don't participate, you may be viewed as an outsider. You can be present because you may be at lunch or at a meeting, but you don't have to be the one saying or fueling all the gossip. Spiteful gossip has a way of swirling around and contaminating a workplace, and in the end, it harms everyone. If you are attuned to Reiki II, put the Cho Ku Rei into the office space, into all four corners of the room, in the lounge and everywhere employees congregate. This symbol will cleanse the room. There will be less gossiping because the negativity won't be there. If your colleagues feel your compassion and good intentions, they will accept and welcome you.

If you aren't attuned to Reiki energy, then you can intend that the workplace be a joyful one, and your altruistic thoughts will automatically come and that in turn will affect all whom you interact with on a daily basis. What we intend becomes reality. If we intend that we will go to work and be stabbed in the back by others and not get recognized for our hard work, then surely, our intentions will become our reality.

Failure is Good!

In your career or for that matter in anything you do, do not become dejected by any failures or rejections that come your way. Usually we fail more than we succeed; however, it only takes one success to eradicate all the past failures. Most successful people have failed a lot, and they don't take these losses personally. Instead they gain immeasurable experience and insight, all of which serve as useful information for their future successes.

Reshma Saujani who founded Girls Who Code (girls who do computer science) says:

FAIL FAST.

FAIL HARD.

FAIL OFTEN.

Saujani is so smart.

Failure just means that you are that much closer to success.

I, for one, don't mind failure because it means that I am engaged and doing the work which is actually the real goal. It's all a process and part of my life.

Gratitude

Be grateful for all that you have.

When you can express and feel genuine appreciation for your life, there is no reason for craving and dissatisfaction. Think about all that you are thankful for such as your loved ones, your home, your health, your relationships, your work, your life and all that it encompasses. This type of thinking is extremely difficult work and it must be done many times a day to change your habitual thought process; however, little by little, you will experience a more peaceful mind and better health.

Possessions

In terms of things, go for less, go for simple. The more you have, the more you have to buy. Use your money for interesting life experiences rather than buying new things. Things have a way of growing and if we become too attached to them, they are a burden instead of their original intent of beauty, of fun, or of making life easier. This is a most valuable lesson to teach to your children and a fighting battle in our society. Be rich with life but keep your things under control if your goal is happiness and peace.

Practice Non-Attachment

What is non-attachment? It is when you lose your favorite watch, and after a brief time of regret and sadness, you are fine without it. You know if you are too attached if you can't stop obsessing about your watch, feeling terrible about the loss.

How do you get unattached to things?

First, remember they are just things. Repeat: they are just things.

It is so interesting to see how some people place an enormous amount of emphasis and importance of having things. Here's a typical person.

This man drives a nice-looking, luxury car. His clothes are of good quality, and he always has the latest model of anything technological. Newest phone? Check. Latest gadget? Check. He's on trend with his lifestyle. If people are frequenting the new restaurant in town, he's right there. He's buying, living, doing whatever is the most popular, the most fashionable. One day, the emptiness will overtake him and he won't know why.

To live like this is soul-less because it has nothing to do with this man as an individual, with his specific interests, needs, ideas and philosophy. He's living for others, for an image.

Put your number one focus on people, specifically your connections to them and the relationships that you have. It is as simple as that. If you do that, you will have exceptional connections and your quality of life will be deeply fulfilling.

Just as important is be non-attached to people. But if you love someone, aren't you attached? Yes, but in a healthy way with clear boundaries. You do not cling, you do not possess, but instead, you allow your person to have space, freedom and the privilege of being the unique human being that she is. This is a most difficult lesson for parents, especially mothers.

Technology and Social Media Create Dissatisfaction

Try to limit your use of technology as it creates havoc, restlessness and dissatisfaction. All the TV shows, the movies, commercials, Facebook, Instagram and Snapchat to name a few, brainwash us into a certain kind of life. For example, most TV shows feature very attractive people. If we watch too much, we may look at ourselves or our partners and feel we are inferior. If we notice their "homes" and how beautiful and luxurious they are, when we survey our own homes, we may think we are not living the right way. It is the same with all material items displayed on the show.

The commercials are the most dangerous because they promote a certain lifestyle and manipulate us strongly into buying. Try putting your TV on mute when the commercials come on, and you will see how peaceful it can be without them. At that time, you can do a few minutes of meditation or just breathe.

Technology use is addictive, and it requires real effort to break away. Do it for your children as you are their role models.

To counteract this media onslaught, increase your time in nature as it will provide balance and calmness. if you don't have opportunities to take a walk at a park or on the beach, then gaze at nature: the sky, your backyard, a flower arrangement, your house plants, a sunrise or sunset, etc.

If you are a gardener, you know how uplifting it is to actually put your hands in soil, touching the earth. It is an amazing grounding and re-centering exercise. You rarely see a gardener steered in the wrong direction.

Ungrateful to the Ones We Love the Most

All the people in your life are important to you. The more you see and interact wth them, the less appreciative you may become of them. Try the Gratitude Exercise on the next page.

Gratitude Exercise

Pick a person who is very close to you. Now imagine that person is no longer in your life. You can make believe that they have moved out of state or the country if the imaginary idea of death is too upsetting.

List all the characteristics you would miss about this person, (e.g. great sense of humor, her tremendous faith in you, his strong character, etc.)

_____

_____

_____

_____

List all the activities that you would miss doing with this person, (e.g. jogging together, dancing/listening to music, golfing, watching sports together and doing other activities, etc.)

_____

_____

_____

_____

Write how your daily life would be changed.

Here's an example from a student:

If I didn't have my husband, I would wake up to an empty house. I would eat breakfast by myself and if there was anything interesting on the news, I wouldn't be able to share it. There would be no reason to save our money for the little trips that we take (we usually plan a few short trips to break up our work schedules) because I would have to take them alone. A lot of the fun is always deciding where to go and then planning it.

During football season, I wouldn't have to grumble because his friends would all be over making a lot of noise. But I would miss that noise and how they always compliment me on the special desserts that I make for them.

Sometimes my husband surprises me with coffee in bed or he'll make a healthy smoothie. I could actually go on and on about all the little things that I would miss about my husband. We always cook together, so I would miss the motivation to cook different food. If he were not in my life, I would be so lonely.

Here's another example from a college student regarding his parents:

Since I went away to college, I began to understand how much my parents mean to me. Mom is just always there, and it's a great feeling that I know I can count on her. For that matter, it is the same with my Dad. Even though I am just an hour away by plane, I don't get a chance to get home very often because of school and my part-time job in a restaurant.

At college, I have to do everything by myself. I didn't realize all the stuff that Mom did. When I do the laundry, make my meals, clean the bathroom, I am aware that all of it was done at home for me. Dad used to help me change the oil in my car, looking for bargains on motor oil. I really miss Dad's grandma's spaghetti sauce that he makes at least once a month. Next time I go home, I'm going to learn how to make it.

The Power of Thank You

We say thank you all the time, it is a basic phrase that pops out automatically that many times we just don't think about it. However, if we thank with true intention, it creates a tremendous energy of joy and of humanness. Try living one day thanking everyone with intention, gratitude and recognition.

There are so many times to say thank you, to remind you of the many gifts that you receive daily. Here are some of those times.

When someone makes:

| you coffee | the bed | a meal |
| an appointment | something for you | etc. |

When someone gives you:

| a gift | a listening ear | her time |
| food | tickets | etc. |

When someone:

takes you anywhere	shares a night out	takes care of your kids
picks up the newspaper	does something nice	drives you somewhere
gives you a neck massage	rubs your feet	fixes something for you
makes your life easier	shows a kindness	compliments you
spends time with you	does you a favor	inspires you
goes out of his way	cooks for you	etc.

If we thank with true gratefulness, it creates a meaningful connection and a spark of joy between the giver and the receiver because the receiver gives back gratitude. Masaru Emoto, the author of *Messages from Water and the Universe*, explains that thoughtful actions/words create gratitude in the receiver which goes back to the initial giver. Emoto puts the ratio of love to gratitude as 1 : 2. For example, 1 is the love (the gift) that is given and the two gratitudes are dispersed with one going back to the original giver as love (the thank you) and then the other gratitude turns into an action of love for another from the receiver and this continues this amazing connection.

Try it with everyone: all your loved ones, your co-workers, your neighbors, the cashier at the market, the coffee barista, the post office worker, the waiter, the bartender, the gardener, the yoga teacher, the car wash worker, your doctor, etc.

Lastly, remember the five principles and reflect upon them daily.

Valerie Dudley, owner of Omni Touch Bodywork in Palm Desert, California, shared that she chooses to turn each principle into a positive affirmation. Here's her meditation.

This day:

I am calm and balanced.

I am at peace.

I am compassionate.

I do my work with honesty and integrity.

I am appreciative, grateful and thoughtful.

The five principles will guide you to live life in a very gracious and meaningful manner.

CHAPTER THREE:
The Value of Meditation

Why is meditation so good for us?

Meditation actually builds brain cells and increases gray matter in the brain. Gray matter is the area which processes information and transports nutrients and energy, helping our brains to function effectively, according to researchers from Harvard University in 2011. In the study, participants who practiced a daily guided meditation had more gray matter in the hippocampi, the parts of the brain which control memory, learning, and self-awareness.

When we meditate, intense gamma waves actually light up the left prefrontal cortex of the brain which relates to cognitive function, an area that actually becomes thinner as we age. Meditation has been proven to thicken the prefrontal cortex; thus, we may be able to navigate old age better.

In turn, meditation decreases the amygdalae, the parts of the brain that are affected by anxiety and stress. The shrinking of the amygdalae indicates that the brain reacts less strongly to stress; therefore, an individual may undergo a high-pressured situation but have less of a negative reaction to it and return back to a calmer state more quickly.

If fear, worry and guilt are present in our minds and bodies, then we will be unable to take whatever action we need. We will be breathing shallowly, so less oxygen will be absorbed into our cells—increasing risk for illness. Also, more possibilities to think incorrectly and to make bad decisions. If less vital oxygen is unavailable to our cells, organs, skin, hair and nails, we will simply be less beautiful! If you can't do meditation for meditation's sake, then do it for vanity!

Physical Benefits

On a physical level, meditation can lower blood pressure and help us to deal better with pain. Many people who suffer from chronic illnesses turn to meditation as a way to manage their symptoms and the helpless feelings they endure. Meditation also strengthens the immune system and decreases the marker C-reactive protein, which is associated with the development of heart disease.

Good and Bad Wandering Minds

Ever hear of monkey mind? This condition is associated with a busy and bouncing mind that is unable to concentrate on anything, thus, causing stress. An overactive default mode network in the brain is the culprit. When we meditate, we quiet the DMN, creating a more peaceful mind. When a person's mind is not jumping from topic to topic, a person feels more relaxed and has better focus.

Moreover, when the PCC (posterior cingulate cortex) increases in gray matter, then so called good mind-wandering activities such as creativity, rumination, self-reflection and the ability to assess one's self in any given situation can come to the forefront. Also, more gray matter in the TPJ, temporo-parietal junction enhances our ability for perspective assessment and more compassion.

A Clear Mind

When we can empty our minds, we give them a much needed rest. In addition, we can reduce fear, worry and guilt and increase possibilities for calmness, relaxation and clarity. It is only then that we can become aware of the endless possibilities that life has to offer, and we will be able to act with focus and a sense of well-being.

If meditation is so good for us, why do so few of us do it?

There may be several contributing factors. Some people say they have tried but can't seem to quiet the mind. Others don't feel that they are doing it correctly. Still, some say that sitting for 20 minutes is impossible.

Beginners might try breathing meditations or guided meditations (many can be found on YouTube) where someone talks you through the meditation). Also, you do not need to sit on the floor. Sitting on a chair works just as well, but remember to always keep the spine straight (to great for developing strong back muscles and aligning your chakras) and the palms resting up to receive. Don't worry about how you are meditating. It will take time for you to feel comfortable and for you to see real results. Measure your progress over time. Ask questions after two weeks, a month, three months, six months, nine months, one year, etc. such as:

Am I more relaxed?

Do I feel better overall?

Am I reacting differently to my problems?

Am I just different?

Do I have more moments of joy?

A common obstacle for beginning meditation is that people are so wound up, caught up in life that they can't relax enough to even try meditating. These people have to wean themselves from excessive use of technology and a busy-busy life. There must be elements of quiet space so that they can create a calmer brain.

To further illustrate, let's use the example of Allison, a woman in her late 20s who works at an advertising agency and who lives with her boyfriend.

Alison's typical day begins at 6:00 am to a blaring alarm clock. She immediately checks her phone even before washing her face. Then she takes the dog out for a quick walk, listening to music on her phone via headphones paying no attention to the trees, landscaped gardens and other surroundings. Often, Alison tunes in to rap or rock to get her energy going.

For breakfast, Alison will grab a protein bar and then head to her favorite coffee house for her morning brew. Three mornings a week, she goes to the gym. During the short drive to the gym, Alison will play more music. At the gym, she will watch a cable show as she runs on the treadmill. Some mornings, she might take an energetic Zumba class.

At work, since Alison's workplace is relatively young, there is always a playlist on as the employers believe that music stimulates creativity (which is a fact but not if it is nonstop).

At lunch, Alison will either brown bag it and if so, she will eat at her desk while scrolling on her phone the entire time. If she does go out, she and a colleague usually hit up a popular restaurant which has a busy vibe and is so loud one has to shout to be heard.

By the end of the day, Alison may either go home with some takeout for her boyfriend or they will meet some friends for happy hour. Again, there is more music, more time on the phone and more shouting to be heard.

At home Alison and her boyfriend will sometimes go on their laptops or watch a show together before they sleep. Even while they watch a show or use the computer, they will constantly check their phones.

How can Alison meditate?

She can't.

Her brain has been inundated all day long plus she is in a high state of agitation. Her day has been focused on digital images. Meditation is just not possible. The only way Alison can even hope to begin a meditation practice is if she starts to find time for quiet space. It is only then that she can be receptive to meditation.

How can people like Alison get quiet?

Ease up on the technology. Cut usage by one third. Too much stimulus creates a busyness in the mind; thus, a restlessness and an inability to focus.

Spend time in nothingness. Dare to be bored. Daily if possible.

Be in nature. Walk in the park, enjoy your backyard or front yard. Gaze at a beautiful sunset, tree or plants.

Do some exercise to expel tension from the body, daily if possible.

Do some breathing exercises, daily if possible.

Make life less busy. Do you really have to go shopping for a new gadget? Do you have to eat out? Do you have to attend that party that you really don't want to go to? Do you have to go from activity to activity from function to function? Do you have to stay up late and watch that show?

Can you talk less and listen more?

Start paying attention to your inner life, not the outside busy/activity life which is what you show to others. Are you doing the things you really want to do? How much are you doing for appearances, for what others may think?

If an individual can do this type of living and breathing for a few weeks, maybe a month, the brain can relax and one can start a meditation practice.

To make meditation a habit, it's best to do it about the same time every day. Purists love the quiet mornings, but do what works for you and your lifestyle. It's your meditation.

After doing breathing and/or guided meditations for a significant time, weeks, months, a year, (whatever is right for you), then start mindful meditation which is when you sit and when a thought appears, you literally push it out of your mind. This type of meditation is very difficult, so again it's best to begin with one minute. Add minutes as you feel comfortable. Practice takes time and effort and consistency. Repeat: One minute is good enough. Do not worry if endless thoughts pop up continuously. Just escort them out.

Meditation is a practice, and it takes a **long time** to feel "successful." By just doing it, you are doing your practice. Be patient, stick to it, and you will get better at it. Through time, you will notice the many benefits: better sleep, better sense of well-being, more patience, the ability for things to roll off your back, more calm, more focus, more tolerance, more compassion, more love and more joy.

Keep in mind that as your meditation practice grows, it will continually evolve. How you meditate now may be very different two years from now. Allow your meditation practice to just be and remain receptive for what comes.

For example, in the early days of my mindful meditation, I would just roll my eyes to the third eye and see a color in my brain. Then I would just push my thoughts out. I did this type of meditation for some time. Then I started to meditate with the image of a white ladder that I would climb inside my mind. When I came to the top, there was a white shelf where I lay down. And weird as this sounds, sometimes Billy Crystal was there waiting for me on my shelf. During those times, we would just sit together and I was always laughing or on the verge of it. Then the shelf evolved into the living room in a white stone modern house where it was open to a beautiful and very blue infinity pool that blended seamlessly into the horizon. Then my meditation was just closing my eyes to the third eye and seeing nothing. That changed back into the white ladder and the modern white stone house again which I use from time to time along with staring into nothing in my mind. This, I am sure, will evolve into something else.

Breathing Exercises

Pay attention to your breathing. When you are stressed out and off track, you will notice that your breath is shallow. Under these circumstances, you will not be able to think clearly as you will be taking in less oxygen. Not surprisingly, people under constant stress are running around breathing from the top of their lungs, making incorrect decisions.

For the following breathing exercises, you can sit on the floor or on a chair, but maintain a straight back without leaning against anything if possible.

Big Belly Breathing

Sit with a straight back.

Place your hands on your belly.

When you inhale, slowly take in oxygen and puff your belly out.

When you exhale, slowly suck your belly in toward your spine.

Do Big Belly Breathing for 30 seconds.

Take a few minutes break and repeat for another 30 seconds.

At first Big Belly Breathing may feel opposite to what you may have been taught— to draw the breath in and suck in your stomach for deep breathing. Big Belly Breathing can be done anywhere, and it resets you to a calmer, more grounded place.

One Two Breathing

One Two Breathing, done only through the nostrils with mouth closed, is not only great preparation for meditation, its mesmerizing breathing and rhythm is a meditation onto itself.

1. Inhale for one.

2. Exhale for two.

3. Inhale for three.

4. Exhale for four.

5. Inhale for five.

6. Exhale for six.

7. Inhale for seven.

8. Exhale for eight.

9. Inhale for nine.

10. Exhale for ten.

Go back to one and repeat entire cycle three times. This technique is excellent when you feel that your mind is racing, and it's also helpful for insomnia as well.

As you get more adept with One Two Breathing, you can play with how long you inhale and exhale. Always inhale/exhale for the same amount of seconds in this meditation. For example, if you breathe in for three seconds, then exhale for three seconds.

Candle Flame Meditation

Sometimes it's helpful to concentrate on a visualization when starting to meditate. For example, you can imagine the flame of a candle in the center of your mind or right in front of you. Here is a meditation that you can try:

1. Sit with your back perfectly straight.

2. Close your eyes and relax by breathing slowly through the nostrils. Do this for about 30 seconds to a minute to get centered.

3. Visualize a candle flame in your mind or in front of you. See the flame flickering. Note the colors. Feel the warmth.

4. See the flame slowly grow larger. Watch as it expands. Perhaps it radiates about your head. Maybe it grows in front of you. It could slowly take over the room or even leave the room. Watch where it goes.

5. Associate joy with the flame as it warms you and everything around you.

6. When you are ready to end the meditation, slowly decrease the flame and bring it back step by step until it is back to its original size.

7. Feel the joy of the candle flame and express your gratefulness. Understand that whenever you want, you can access the candle flame and its warmth, feeling joy and peace.

I like to do this meditation on winter days because it seems to actually warm me up.

Mindful Meditation

1. Sit on a chair with feet flat on the floor or sit on the floor with legs crossed. In either position, maintain a perfectly straight back.

2. Rest your palms face up either in your lap or on your thighs.

3. Close your eyes.

4. Start by breathing slowly through the nose, slow inhalations and exhalations. Your mouth is closed. Do this until you feel that you have slowed down, for 20-60 seconds.

5. Pay attention to your body, noting any tensions. Perhaps it's in your neck or lower back. Release the tensions by imagining that you are breathing into those tight areas. When you inhale, see a color such as pink fill your neck area, and as you exhale, see the pink slowly dissolve. Repeat this technique a few times until you feel less tension.

6. Now set a timer for one minute. Roll your eyes upward to the third eye, that point on your forehead just above the brow which stimulates intuition. Close your eyes and keep them rolled to the third eye. (If you are uncomfortable rolling your eyes up to the third eye, then just don't do it.)

7. Start the meditation. When a thought enters your mind, acknowledge it and let it go. Be patient. Keep on repeating this technique until the timer goes off.

Daily Meditation Breaks

Life can be a meditation if you approach it by using meditation throughout your day. For example, right before you start your car, take ten seconds to just close your eyes and to feel your breathing. If you ride public transportation, it's so simple to close your eyes for a few seconds to become self-aware.

Look for opportunities throughout the day to take a mini-meditation break.

It can be:

at the gym	while you brush your teeth	at school
at the store	before the church sermon	before a test
as you pump gas	in front of the computer	when you get a manicure
in the shower	in line at the coffeehouse	in the movie theater
as you make coffee	before a meeting	at work
at the bank	while you are on hold	on the golf course
in an elevator	when you're stuck in traffic	as you wash dishes
in front of the TV	while the microwave is on	before you sleep
	even on the toilet!	

Absolutely Anywhere You Are!

Your brain will appreciate these tiny pit-stops throughout the day, and all these breaks will add up to enhance your meditation practice.

CHAPTER FOUR:
The Chakras

It is important to understand the chakra system and how it works because several of the Reiki hand positions work over the chakras.

What are chakras?

Chakras are energy centers on the outer body that allow life energy to flow in and out of the auras. Sometimes they become imbalanced due to a multitude of problems—childhood issues, lifestyle choices, thought patterns, life stresses, etc.

The goal is to keep our chakras healthy and balanced. Reiki is one way to do this, but there are many other healing modalities that are also effective. Some of these include: acupuncture, acupressure, Shiatsu, as well as yoga, tai chi, and qi gong. Breathing exercises and meditation are also effective, especially when the breath and intent is directed toward specific chakras.

Here are just some of the physical, mental and emotional issues associated with the seven main chakras.

1st Chakra, the root, red

Location: The perineum, the base of the spine, extends to our legs and feet.

Physical: Bones, teeth, elimination system, large intestine, adrenal glands, sciatica, gout.

Mental: Materialistic, wanting to hoard. Not trusting and feeling a lack of belonging or connection to others.

Emotional: Insecure, anxious and nervous.

Financial problems and basic survival are associated with this chakra. When 1st chakra is balanced, we feel grounded and secure.

2nd Chakra, the sacral, orange

Location: Above the root chakra up to just under the navel.

Physical: Lower digestive tract, reproductive organs, bladder, kidneys, prostate,
           infertility, sexual dysfunction, difficult periods.

Mental: Unable to accept personal pleasure. May look to be offended.

Emotional: Jealous and possessive. May be over-attached to people, to things and to
           situations. Can be over-emotional or repressed in expression.

Ease of relationships, creativity and healthy sexuality are all part of the 2nd chakra. We
store our first impressions and old emotional "movies" here.

3rd Chakra, the solar plexus, yellow

Location: Above the 2nd chakra up until under the chest.

Physical: Liver, gall bladder, stomach, spleen, small intestine, pancreas.

Mental: Domineering or too indecisive, always second guessing. Over-confident
         or lacking confidence. Manipulative, power-hungry, poor self-discipline.

Emotional: Feeling egotistical or inferior.

The third chakra is all about self-identity, one's strength and will.

4th Chakra, the heart, green and can be pink

Location: The chest, shoulders, arms and hands.

Physical: Heart, lungs and thymus gland.

Mental: Trust issues, selfishness, fear of intimacy.

Emotional: Coldness, distant or suffocating love. Over-sacrificing to the point of
            neglecting self, being the martyr.

The ability to be open to new people and experiences are signs of a balanced 4th chakra.
A person who can view himself and others compassionately has a balanced heart chakra.

48

5th Chakra, the throat, sky blue

Location: The throat, neck and mouth

Physical: Larynx, thyroid gland, the voice, cervical vertebrae.

Mental: Honest and clear communication patterns, fear of confrontations/discussions.

Emotional: Panic attacks. Talking too much or too little are results of an emotional imbalance as well as the inability to listen to one's self and others.

A balanced 5th chakra also is the ability to be creative. One doesn't have to do art but one can live creatively in solving problems for example. Resonance in one's voice.

6th Chakra, the third eye, indigo

Location: Just above the space between the eyebrows on the forehead.

Physical: Migraines, brain, eye, ears and nose, pituitary gland, hormonal function.

Mental: Ability to think for one's self, does not have to rely too much on authority.

Emotional: Veers to fantasy to deal with life.

A balanced 6th chakra indicates an understanding as to how life works. One feels intuitive and has clarity as to how one fits into the scheme of life.

7th Chakra, the crown, violet and can be white

Location: Right above the top of the head.

Physical: Sleep disorders, brain problems, depression, dizziness, pineal gland.

Mental: Prejudiced, intellectualizes everything, a lack of faith in life.

Emotional: Confusion, indecision, rigid and sometimes over-attached.

It is at the 7th chakra where we seek spirituality and expansion of our souls.

For an in-depth study, read *Wheels of Life* by Anodea Judith, a renown chakra expert.

Seven Main Chakras

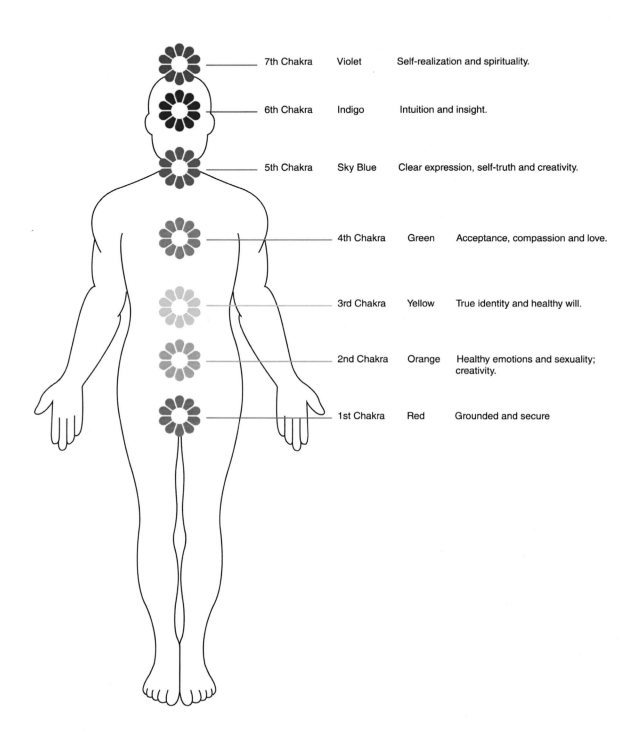

7th Chakra	Violet	Self-realization and spirituality.
6th Chakra	Indigo	Intuition and insight.
5th Chakra	Sky Blue	Clear expression, self-truth and creativity.
4th Chakra	Green	Acceptance, compassion and love.
3rd Chakra	Yellow	True identity and healthy will.
2nd Chakra	Orange	Healthy emotions and sexuality; creativity.
1st Chakra	Red	Grounded and secure

Development of Chakras

The seven chakras are developed during specific periods in childhood from the womb to early adulthood. Although the chakras are activated at that time, a person can nurture and balance them at any time.

What may be revealing and insightful is if a person explores his childhood to early adulthood, he may find key milestones and significant events that shaped his development. For example, one person may recall her father's death at age five (heart chakra development). Perhaps, that is why this person is afraid of being vulnerable and breaks up with people before they become too close to her. This kind of information can be most valuable in a person's healing journey.

Another person sees that at age three, he was given the responsibility of taking care of the family's pet rabbit. Although he did not realize that his parents were monitoring him, he remembers feeling vey proud and important at that young age. Perhaps his current third chakra strength—strong leadership ability—can be attributed to the self esteem he developed at that young age.

The following developmental times are from Anodea Judith in her book *Eastern Body Western Mind.*

First Chakra

Mid-Pregnancy to 12 months

Formation of physical body, bones and teeth.

Survival and physical body health.

Trust vs. Mistrust.

Affirms right to be here.

Relates to body, family life, money issues.

How to develop first chakra?

Emotional state of mother is very important during pregnancy. Is the baby wanted?

Provide nurturing and peaceful environment. Extra nurturing if child goes to day care.

Answer baby's cries. Baby should feel safe and not left to cry alone by herself.

Baby should not be separated from parents (especially mother) for long periods of time.

Second Chakra

6 months to 2 years

Feeling and mobility, understanding separateness.

Communication through emotions; parents acknowledging baby's feelings.

Relates to emotional and sexual health and creativity.

How to develop second chakra?

Allow child to explore yet feel safe with parent nearby.

When child expresses an emotion, acknowledge it and explain how to deal with it in very simple terms, (i.e. let chid cry, get mad, feel sad). Do not push emotions under the rug.

Show child how to enjoy life by being playful, showing joy and laughter.

Third Chakra

18 months to about 4 years old

Development of will.

Self power but do not allow child to have more power than parent.

Formation of ego identity.

Allow experimentation.

How to develop third chakra?

Allow child to take age appropriate risks.

Give age-appropriate tasks so child feels sense of accomplishment. (e.g. Let child throw away litter, put toy back in closet, etc. Involves parent's patience because these chores will take more time.)

Encourage independence; do not over-manage everything.

Do not make love contingent upon child's obedience.

Allow child's time table for toilet training.

Try to limit criticisms.

Let child make his own decisions (when appropriate and safe) and learn consequences from them.

Fourth Chakra

4 - 7 years

Understanding relationships.

Interest in friends outside of family.

Formation of social identity, wanting to fit in.

How to develop fourth chakra?

Encourage friendships.

Model healthy relationships.

Welcome people into your home.

Do volunteer work together.

Model empathy and thoughtfulness to your child and others.

Explain and demonstrate how to forgive.

Be open to new people and new experiences.

Fifth Chakra

7 - 12 years

Creative expression.

Expansion and experimentation.

Self-express through communication.

How to develop fifth chakra?

Support natural curiosity and creativity.

Appreciate child's work and accomplishments.

Expose child to greater world through books, movies, field trips, travel, etc.

Speak honestly and express thoughts well.

Allow child to state his opinion without criticism.

Parents make sure that what they say aligns with what they do.

Sixth Chakra

Adolescence

Re-examining social identity and making changes.

Inner sight or illusion.

How to develop sixth chakra?

Maintain stable home life for the rocky, teen years.

Maintain clear boundaries.

Support independence and safe experimentation.

Allow child to make changes to his appearance as long as they are not dangerous or unethical to your family's values.

Model taking time for reflection.

Show teen how to trust her own judgment and intuition.

Seventh Chakra

Early adulthood and beyond.

Pursuit of knowledge.

Formation of a world view and how one fits in.

Comprehension of life.

How to develop seventh chakra?

Promote life learning.

Demonstrate observational skills in life.

Continue to expose the spiritual side of life.

Practice meditation.

Emphasize life acceptance.

Open mind to new ways of thinking.

Now that you have learned the key times in childhood and early adulthood when chakras activate, take a look at your life. Try to recall as many important events in your life—milestones, special accomplishments, sad times, family situations, etc.

Some examples:

Death of a loved one.

Marriage or divorce.

Remarriage of parents.

Birth of a sibling.

An important achievement such as winning something, making the team, voted class president, etc.

Time when you met your best friend or lost a friendship.

A humiliating experience or a moment of extreme recognition.

Moving to a new home, city, state, or country.

Parent losing a job and the aftermath.

Failing a class or getting high honors.

Beginning a strong interest such as music, sports, dance, chess, etc.

Getting your first job.

A serious illness to you or your loved one.

Any major family issue.

These are just some ideas to help you brainstorm. Perhaps, today you will only think of some key times in your life. Later, however, you may be reminded of other events which may provide greater understanding on how your specific chakras developed.

Write them down on the Life Event Chart on the next page.

Life Event Chart

1st Chakra: Mid-pregnancy - 12 months

_____

_____

_____

2nd Chakra: 6 months - 2 years

_____

_____

_____

3rd Chakra: 18 months - 4 years

_____

_____

_____

4th Chakra: 4 years - 7 years

_____

_____

_____

5th Chakra: 7 years - 12 years

_____

_____

_____

6th Chakra: Adolescence

_____

_____

_____

7th Chakra: Adulthood and Beyond

_____

_____

_____

Restoring Chakra Balance

A strong Reiki practice as well as other healing modalities can restore chakra balance. These methods all share the principle that when the life force in our bodies is free flowing and clear, disease cannot thrive.

Sometimes it's just a matter of putting your attention on a specific chakra to clear it. Other times, blocks can run deep, and it may take a long time and a combination of different healing modalities to heal. Our lives are not static. That is why we are always evolving and thus our chakras constantly move in and out of balance. Follow a healthy daily routine and do what is necessary for you to remain clear.

Here are just some of the ways to rebalance the chakras.

First Chakra

Chant the mantra Lam (pronounced Lahm) daily.

Do a grounding activity such as yoga or tai chi.

Garden—touch the soil.

Walk barefoot outside.

Incorporate red into your life—wear it, drink out of a red mug, use a red pen, etc.

Connect with nature.

Eat nourishing stews, hearty breads, oatmeal—food with substance.

Make your home environment cozy and welcoming.

Some yoga poses: mountain, easy sitting, all warrior and balancing asanas.

Second Chakra

Chant the mantra Vam (pronounced Vahm) daily.

Incorporate orange into your life—wear it, eat it, get orange towels, orange accessories, etc.

Release and express your emotions.

Fulfill desires and make room for pleasure.

Leave the past where it is—just use for information and comprehension.

Make sure water intake is sufficient and do water sports such as swimming, etc.

Re-evaluate your sex attitudes—guilt has no place.

Activities involving movement such as exercise, dance, are all good.

Explore creativity in all that you do and think.

Some yoga poses: pigeon and goddess.

Third Chakra

Chant the mantra Ram (pronounced Rahm) daily.

Challenge yourself by taking a small risk out of your comfort zone.

Incorporate yellow into your life—wear it, paint a room, get a yellow hat, etc.

Accept who you are and change what you don't like.

Set a small daily goal and fulfill it.

Have patience with yourself.

Carbohydrates (in moderation) provide energy and stamina.

Some yoga poses: plank and boat.

Fourth Chakra

Chant the mantra Yam (pronounced Yahm) daily.

Open your heart to new people and new experiences.

Incorporate green in your life—plants, clothing (especially blouses, shirts, tops, jackets and sweater since they all are worn over the heart chakra).

Be compassionate to yourself first.

Practice loving-kindness meditation.

Don't put your relationships under a microscope.

Eat more vegetables.

Do aerobic exercise so you work out the lungs.

Do breathing exercises.

Some yoga poses: cobra, camel, and fish.

Fifth Chakra

Chant the mantra Ham (pronounced Hahm) daily.

Listen to your communication and others'.

Incorporate blue into your life—wear it, live in it, drive it, etc.

Listen to music.

Sing, chant and hum.

Do what you say you will do.

Speak truthfully and know your truth.

Find your creative expression.

Eat more fruit.

Some yoga poses: plow and shoulder stand.

Sixth Chakra

Say the mantra aum (pronounced Ahm) daily.

Roll your eyes to the third eye and meditate on it.

Incorporate indigo into your life—wear it, live with it, etc.

Cultivate intuition.

Take time for self-reflection.

Try to recall dreams and write them down.

Journal regularly.

Do daily meditation.

Seventh Chakra

Chant the mantra Om (pronounced Ohm).

Incorporate violet into your life and environment.

Live a present-oriented life.

Practice non-attachment to people, things, situations, state of mind.

Learn and study.

Practice self care on a mature and consistent level.

Every now and then, fast—can just be a dinner-less day.

Observe to understand.

Embrace spirituality.

Just be.

Balancing our chakras is not easy because life is always happening. However, if we understand our chakras, then we know how to reset ourselves whenever we become imbalanced. It can be as simple as doing a breathing technique or opening ourselves to new experiences.

If you are too busy to think about all the ways to balance your chakras, adopt a regular yoga practice to bring chakras into equilibrium. You can also try Chakra Mantra Meditation on the next page.

Chakra Mantra Meditation

Sound mediation has a very healing effect on the mind and body. It starts deep with our most inner being and radiates through our cells, organs and body to even our etheric body (in our aura where the chakras lie).

Each chakra has a sound which when chanted can help balance it. You can chant all the sounds or just hone in on the ones which you may feel need more help. All of the sounds except for om (ohm) have a short "a" sound, so lam would be lahm.

1st	root chakra for survival, feeling grounded and secure	lam
2nd	sacral chakra for healthy emotions, sexuality and creativity	vam
3rd	solar plexus chakra for true identity and healthy will	ram
4th	heart chakra for acceptance, compassion and ability to love	yam
5th	throat chakra for clear expression, self-truth and creativity	ham
6th	third eye chakra for intuition, pure thought and insight	aum
7th	crown chakra for self-realization and spirituality	om

* Sometimes the 6th chakra is om as well as the 7th.

There are many other mantras to try. Some of them are rooted in yoga such as Om Mane Padme Hum which works on transforming one's impure mind/body/soul into purity. This mantra also helps to build compassion.

You can also create your own mantra. Perhaps you are working on having more peace in your life. You can simply say "Peace" over and over again. You can draw the word out. Maybe you want to use "Live well." You can use your imagination and specifically cater it to your own needs and life. Some other ideas for mantras: Breathe, Think, Be Wise, Just Love, Just Be, Why Not, Laugh, Smile, etc.

CHAPTER FIVE:
Understanding Ourselves

To understand ourselves is to see ourselves with clarity and honesty. Many times, we are a stranger to ourselves. We can't see ourselves without prejudice. Our point of view is the only one, the right one, so we discredit and ignore others and their ideas.

How do we get past this wall of ignorance?

We first have to accept that we may have false illusions, that our reality may not be absolutely true. Or put it this way: It is true for us, but not necessarily for everyone else.

Next, we must explore who we truly are and that entails an exploration into our childhoods and family style. We won't dwell on the past, but we will use that information as knowledge of life experience.

Lastly, we open our minds through meditation, clearing ourselves of life's debris in order that we can start this point in our lives, fresh, focused and clear.

Family Legacy and Family Patterns

It's important to understand that we are first products of our environment and our family legacy. If we look closely at families, it's evident that certain patterns run through them. One family may have a history of being sociable hosts yet has a multi-generational struggle with alcohol. Another family may be shy and carry that reserve, yet be of sound character. There may be a family whose members have violent tempers yet support each other 100 percent. Another family may be plagued with infidelity, and rampant breakups of marriages and relationships.

All families have a beauty and a special uniqueness; yet, all families are flawed. It is up to us to identify our family's weaknesses, to do our very best to address them so that they do not continue into the next generation. The goal is to always help the next generation to be better by being the beneficiaries of our life experiences and wisdom.

Who are you?

Write a short paragraph about who you believe you are. For example, are you a go-getter determined to get your goals? Or are you an easy-going person who likes to enjoy life? Are you generous? Are you fearful? Write as if you were describing yourself to another person.

Here is my example:

I am a person who believes she is fair-minded, and I want other people to see me that way. I dislike bragging and try to practice humility, a characteristic not really respected in today's culture. I can be very impatient and too quick to see the faults of others, forgetting that I am the same. I can be friendly in the way children are friendly and have to remind myself that most adults are not like this and will be made uncomfortable. I can be insecure about myself and my abilities, but other times I am pleased which shows my contradictory nature. I can be emotional yet I can also detach and watch my life and others like a movie. I can be demanding of my loved ones, but on occasion, I can be blind to their needs. I can be extremely kind and other times, quite dense. My sense of humor is off the charts as I can usually see the funny side in anything. I rarely get embarrassed; thus, I forget that others may embarrass more easily. I can sense others' pain, so I have to be careful to whom I choose to be around. I believe in trying my best with people and in this way, I rarely feel guilty or regretful as I know at that time, I did my best even if it was not good enough. I am highly opinionated but most people will never know because I don't feel it's necessary to reveal myself completely. I believe we all have a purpose to help each other and that all the things we do in our lives have more impact and power than we think or will ever know.

Seeing Yourself Without Prejudice

It is so very difficult to see ourselves without prejudice. Yet, it is a very important factor for our healing, and by stripping away our layers to our true selves, we can experience more beautiful and easier lives because we understand our true natures.

This survey can be a learning experience if you can look at it without bias. First, you will fill it out and then you will ask three people to fill the surveys out. You can select a very close person, a person in your circle and then a neighbor or colleague at work. Ask them to fill them out quickly, not over thinking the exercise. They should not write their names on the survey. Just fold their survey and put it into a folder. Don't look at the surveys until you have all three in your possession.

On a scale of 1 - 5 with 1 being the lowest and five the highest, rate the following:

1.   How considerate is this person?   _____

2.   How good a listener? _____

3.   How often does this person brag? _____

4.   How generous? _____

5.   How envious? _____

6.   How helpful? _____

7.   How selfish? _____

8.   How compassionate? _____

9.   How ambitious? _____

10.   How responsible? _____

11.   How dependent? _____

12.   How humorous? _____

13. How negative? _____

14. How positive? _____

15. How energetic? _____

16. How greedy? _____

17. How angry? _____

18. How grateful? _____

19. How judgmental? _____

20. How confident? _____

21. How lazy? _____

22. How friendly? _____

23. How mentally strong? _____

24. How fearful? _____

25. How defensive? _____

For each question, add up each question and average them. For example, for question number one, How considerate is this person, add up all three survey responses. Perhaps, one person gave a three and the other two people, a score of four. So add 4 + 4 + 3 = 11. Divide the total 11 by 3 so that would equal 3.66 which can be rounded up to a four. Now compare that number to your answer. If you gave yourself a three, then you can see that others view you as more thoughtful. If you gave yourself a 1, then you know that you may have been too harsh.

Reflect on all that you have learned.

Our Thought Process

Everything we do and say and even more importantly, everything we think creates the energy that we experience. If we think a daily diet of negative thoughts, that energy will harm us physically, mentally and emotionally. We may get ill or put ourselves in harm's way. Pessimism can hurt our relationships and harmful thoughts can trigger the wrong kind of behavior.

The next time you get an ache in your body, a cold or something minor that prevents you from being 100%, ask these questions:

Is something or someone bothering me?

Have I done something or think myself wrong?

Am I repeatedly thinking about a hurtful experience, past, present or future?

Try accepting whatever happened. Acknowledge that if someone hurt you or if you are the offending party, that you and the other person are just human, making a human mistake. Give the other party or yourself a free pass if this is not consistent behavior and forgive that person or yourself.

Acknowledge that repetitive negative thinking is destructive to good health.

It is said that we think over 60,000 thoughts a day and even if a third is negative, that is about 20,000 too many!! It's important to think good thoughts to create a mental attitude that will benefit us in our health, well-being and social interactions. It is not helpful to be critical of ourselves and others. We will lose out in warm relationships and the ability to create a life of deep connections. Critical people do not have good friendships; how can they? Who wants to be around unsupportive people? We must be accepting of ourselves and others.

Write down the three negative thoughts that are currently in your mind. Don't overthink this exercise, just do it.

1. _____

2. _____

3. _____

It is so easy to think negative thoughts. It is part of our human mind and the conditioning that we undergo in life. As children, we are innocent and do not have the burdens of life experience. Therefore, young minds are lighter in thinking and optimism is very high as opposed to the adult mind which has had its share of life's hurts and disappointments. Then we learn to think defensively to protect ourselves against possible negative results.

How do we counteract this harmful thought process?

When we think a negative thought, we immediately turn the thought into a more positive one. It's a retraining of the mind and if done enough, the positive thought will arise more readily than the negative one. We ask ourselves simple questions such as what Dr. Anthony Komaroff, physician/professor at Harvard Medical School, wrote in one of his newspaper columns in 2016:

Is this thought or belief true?

Did I jump to a conclusion?

What evidence do I actually have?

What's the worst that could happen?

How else can I think about this?

Here are some examples of negative thoughts and how to change them.

Example: I am angry at my best friend for forgetting my birthday.

Instead think: This is the first time in five years that she has forgotten. What is going on in her life? How can I be helpful? Did I do something to hurt her? I'm going to ask her.

Example: I am not that smart.

Instead think: I may not be a genius, but I am knowledgeable about some things. I can read, take classes and learn new things. I can change my attitude to appreciate what I have and share that with others.

Example: I'll never have a good relationship.

Instead think: I am a good person with a lot to offer. I can focus on bettering myself in so many ways. I can become healthier and thus more attractive. I can think well so my energy is high.

Now go back to the three negative thoughts that you wrote down. Cross them out and change them to be more constructive.

Do this type of thinking daily. Cross out your negative thoughts and change them. It is very difficult and not always possible. However, if you persist, you will see how this type of thinking becomes a habit. Next, do the Childhood Reflection exercise to gain a little insight into your childhood. It will start you thinking about how your childhood really was. Then look to see if you have made strides and changes, or you simply replicating your childhood without much thought? Have you replaced any negative behaviors for positive ones? Or perhaps this exercise will make you more aware; thus, you can begin to live more consciously and constructively.

Childhood Reflection

Take time to think about your childhood. Circle all words that describe your childhood.

confusion	laughter	depression	nurturing	optimistic	communicative
negligent	shyness	distant	insecure	loving	coldness
supportive	pessimistic	closeness	alcohol	drugs	lonely
secure	fun times	controlled	broken	warm	creative
chaotic	pretension	peaceful	assertive	freedom	unfaithful
trusting	content	sad	passive	honest	togetherness
strict	hateful	safe	tears	humorous	money woes
clean	cluttered	selfish	nervous	jealousy	loyal
anger	silent	calm	affectionate	broken	perfectionism
anxious	attached	proper	negligent	dramatic	quiet
great vacations	lovely home environment		quiet	discussions	put downs

Now write down all the words that describe your life now. How many are the same?

How many are different? Here's the chance to take a clear look as to how our lives are progressing and how to make appropriate changes.

Intuition

Intuition is a sense that is not highly used anymore. There was a time when people lived with nature and had simpler yet physically more demanding lives. People lived in accordance with the land and their instinctive nature was sharp. They paid attention to the weather and seasons, to the animals and plants in their environment, all helping them to make crucial daily-life decisions.

However, for those of us who live in urban areas, our lifestyles are fast-paced and technology dominated. We cannot listen because we have all these distractions in the way, blocking us from the intuition connection.

Little children, especially babies and very young children, are quite intuitive because that is all they know. Observe them. They instinctively know what to do—how to nurse from their mother, when to cry if they are hungry or when to withdraw. They know whom they like and will simply not go to people who make them uncomfortable.

It's difficult to say when children lose their intuitive nature, but it is when they understand that their actions are perceived and judged by others. They rein in their impulses and adapt their behavior towards their peers and adults. They desire acceptance and as children grow, they learn to seek what our society promotes: power and prestige.

When people fixate on these superficial goals, they stop trusting their intuition because they don't see it as a way to achieve them. Besides in our scrambling to reach the top, life is so chaotic and noisy that we cannot hear intuition even if we wanted to.

How to Cultivate Intuition

A daily meditation practice is key to getting our intuition back. If we can get quiet enough, then intuition can come to the forefront. A busy busy busy life will cloud intuition. Life will be just one big reaction, and we will feel out of control, dissatisfied and unhappy.

When our intuition is working properly, it is like having a direct link to the center of the universe. How we should live our lives is crystal clear. We don't have doubts because we just know. Our relationships work better and we make less mistakes. Our work flows because we are doing the correct work. It is at this time that our wisdom can grow.

Most of us are off track. We are products of our families, our environment and society. We do things because they are mainstream, considered the norm, and expected. We fear being different because then we may not be accepted by others.

The need for acceptance is probably one of the key basic needs for all humans. This need is so powerful that it can blind us to who we really are. When we really investigate people whose lives are fascinating and fulfilling, almost always, they have decided to listen to their inner voice, no matter how unpopular or difficult their choices may be. People in their sphere tell them that their ideas/goals are ridiculous and just not possible. Somehow, these individuals persevere on despite any lack of support. Like a homing pigeon, these people follow their own inner guidance and are richer for it.

If you look around your various circles of family, friends and acquaintances, you may be surprised to see that there are people that you know, living fulfilling lives, following their own guidelines and ideals.

Meditation and Reiki can help retrieve intuition and bring it to fruition. A daily meditation practice will quiet your mind, and with a quieter mind, you will be able to listen well.

Having intuition is an incredible gift that is always present for you to utilize. Every situation or problem can be "solved." Intuition brings a sense of peace that if you just listen, you will understand and know who you are and how to proceed with your life.

Intuition Exercise

I wrote the following exercise effortlessly and later when I recently re-read renown yogi Erich Schiffman's book, *Yoga The Spirit and Practice of Moving into Stillness*, I realized that I was totally influenced by his wisdom over 20 years ago when I first read his book. His words became so ingrained in me that I thought they were my original ideas. Instead, I can say with truth that this exercise was totally inspired by him!

After you have woken up and finished your morning rituals and meditation, try to ask yourself these questions.

What shall I eat for breakfast?

Eat whatever comes to mind first.

What shall I wear today?

Wear whatever comes to mind. You can ask for your entire outfit, or just ask what shirt to wear or what shoes.

Which way should I commute today?

Sometimes we have a choice as to what freeway, what street or what bus/train to take.

Throughout the day, ask yourself some of these questions and listen for the first answer. Write it down if that's convenient, so you don't get confused with other answers that quickly come to mind.

Who is calling me?

What movie should I see?

Should I make a right turn or a left turn?

Should I go down this aisle for a parking space?

Should I go out with this person?

Do I like this person?

Will it be cold tomorrow?

Should I go to that party?

Should I take this class?

Is this person lying to me?

As you can see, there are as many questions as there are seconds in a day. (Of course, you don't want to spend your entire day asking questions for everything.) The key is to honor any answer you receive. If your intuition tells you to order the pasta special for lunch rather than the chicken sandwich, then choose the pasta. By following your intuition, you will be rewarded by gaining better insight. Intuition grows with use.

By practicing intuition on the silly trivial things in life, when the big important decisions come up, you will be able to hear more effectively.

Little by little, your intuition will get stronger. You may have an urge to call someone you haven't talked to in a long time. You may find out that the person is ill or in need of something. In your life, you may find so many situations—trivial or very important—where your intuition has guided you correctly.

Intuition is a gift. it brings a sense of personal strength and knowledge that you can always listen for your truth and that you will be living your best life.

When you hear your intuition, trust it and act accordingly.

CHAPTER SIX:
The Daily Routine

1. How is your daily nutrition? What are the good foods that you eat? What are the bad foods?

2. How is your water intake? Can you improve?

3. What kind of exercise routine do you have? What could you do to make it better?

4. How is your breathing? Do you do any breathing exercises?

5. Do you have a meditation practice? How often and for how long?

6. How do you relax?

7. Do you think good encouraging thoughts about yourself and others?

The Need For a Strong Daily Routine

To have a fulfilling and meaningful life, there must be some order and regularity. When the basics of life are well taken care of and done well, then a person is not only free to focus on her dreams, but she will be at her best physically, mentally, and emotionally.

If you look at well-known artists, musicians and writers from the past, most of them maintained a daily regimen in order to work successfully on their craft. For example, the composer Franz Schubert was at his desk at 6:00 am every morning and worked until 1:00 pm. Then he would go to a coffee house where he smoked and read newspapers.

The artist Georgia O'Keefe lived a more solitary but fulfilling existence in the New Mexico desert with just a few people coming into her daily sphere. She was either spending her days painting or maintaining her garden and answering mail. (*Daily Rituals: How Artists Work* by Mason Currey, Knopf 2013).

Other artists worked regularly but lived hard, drinking and carousing at night (Ernest Hemingway and Jackson Pollock for example). However, they still kept to their working schedules despite their excesses. Hopefully, we can just adopt their work ethic.

Our daily habits are the important factors that contribute to an overall healthy life. Of course, we will sometimes overindulge or be unable to maintain our healthy regimen; however, if we can more or less stay on course, be regular in our eating, exercise, meditation, thinking and relaxing routines, we have a good chance of maintaining our physical, mental and emotional health. Good health equals success in anything that we choose to do.

Tracking Moods

When you practice good self-care, you will naturally just feel better, more satisfied and in control of your life which leads to greater happiness.

Before attempting to change your daily routine, track your moods for about two weeks. On a calendar, rank how you feel at the end of each day by rating it from 1-5 with 1 being a dismal mood while 5 being spectacular.

After you have recorded your moods for two weeks, start making the little changes to your daily routine. Once you have spent a month in a healthier routine, start tracking how you feel again for two weeks. Now compare your new moods to your earlier moods prior to your daily routine makeover. The difference may be significant.

Healthy Eating

Our first priority is balanced and healthy nutrition. Freshly prepared food featuring a variety of vegetables, grains and fruit is optimal. Think about the nutritious foods that you eat daily. What are they?

If you aren't eating healthily, commit to one nutritious item each day. Make and honor that commitment. Perhaps, you will eat a salad or have an apple. Maybe you eat a small packet of almonds and raisins or steam some vegetables.

Now think of the "bad" foods that you eat daily. What are they? Chances are they are food from outside the home or food that comes in a box or package that contains chemicals and preservatives. Processed food is the absolute enemy to good health. However, if you are going to eat food that comes in boxes or packages, make sure that the food is minimally processed. For example, buy potato chips that list the ingredients: potatoes, oil and salt. You can always find a healthier alternative. Eliminate one bad food a day and honor that commitment.

Too Much Sugar

An excess of sugar can slow down the growth of neurotrophins in the brain. We need neurotrophins to help grow new neurons, brain cells. When the brain burns glucose (fruit, sugar and carbohydrates), like a car there is an exhaust, free radicals, which can interfere with the signals the brain sends throughout the body. Our bodies make antioxidants which can cancel out the free radicals. But if we eat too much sugar and white flour carbohydrates, the excess free radicals can create depression, anxiety and other diseases. What happens when we are depressed or anxious? Our feel good levels of serotonin and dopamine plunge, and we usually reach for comfort food, such as carbohydrates and sweets. Our food choices create more inflammation in the gut and send stress signals to the brain, producing more free radicals, creating a vicious cycle. Antioxidants such as vitamins C, E, beta carotene and flavonoids have been shown to help prevent and repair free radicals. Next time, you feel emotionally down, push yourself to reach for whole grains, fruit, vegetables, tea and nuts instead.

Phytonutrients

Vitamins and supplements are helpful, but fresh fruits and vegetables are better because not only do they contain vitamins but many phytonutrients as well. Phytonutrients are the natural chemicals found in plant foods and also in whole grains, nuts, beans and teas. Their importance is to help our cells to communicate well, so that proper function and reactions take place.

Too much consumption of vitamins rather than the actual food means that we will miss out on these valuable phytonutrients as well as the fiber. For example, resveratrol, found in blueberries and red wine among other plant foods, helps to protect skin and is an antioxidant. It also reduces inflammation and may lower risk of heart disease and some cancers.

In addition, carrots have carotenoids which are antioxidants that tackle harmful free radicals. Some of them can be converted to Vitamin A which is great for the immune system and for eye health. Another carotenoid is lycopene which is found in tomatoes and may lower risk in prostate cancer, while lutein and zeaxanthin help with cataracts and macular degeneration.

There are literally thousands of phytonutrients and more are being discovered. Use vitamins and supplements as added support, not as a replacement for healthy eating.

I came to care about cooking because of a situation that occurred when our family traveled to Iran one summer when our daughter was one and half years old. At that time, I hated to cook and resented it. My husband came from a culture that traditionally cooks fresh food every day, and our marriage is more traditional in the sense that I do all the cooking. (I had seen my Japanese mother do all the cooking when I was growing up that I didn't even think about sharing meal preparations. Of course, I raised my daughter to think differently!)

My food prior to Iran was bland, boring and prepared haphazardly. My husband was always doctoring up my food with salt and spices, and since he did not want to take over the culinary duties, that is how we ate.

In Iran, my sister-in-law learned that my daughter loved pasta, so she set about making it for lunch. I watched as my sister-in-law diced onions and garlic and sautéed them until they were translucent. Next, she added some ground beef and really took her time breaking up the chunks of meat. "To be a good cook, you must be patient," she said in her fluent English. Then she added tomato paste but she actually sautéed the paste first to bring out the flavor, pushing the onions and meat to the side. I don't remember what else she added, but I do recall a squeeze of lemon amidst the different seasonings.

I watched with fascination as it was a cooking tutorial deserving to be on Food Network. However, what really sold me was how my daughter just scarfed up that pasta, eating joyfully with her hands and smacking her lips. Moreover, this was her experience with all the food in Iran, and it totally opened my eyes. Of course, my daughter didn't eat my food with joy—how could she as I could barely stomach it myself.

When I returned back home, I resolved to be a better cook, and it really just required a commitment and openness to learning. Today some 20 years later, it is so wonderful when my daughter and husband compliment my food. Best of all, I learned to love cooking, and it's been an important part of my daily routine. I find the act of chopping, sautéing, mixing—all to be very meditative and the knowledge that I am serving the best possible nutrients to my family and myself, satisfies and gives me a sense of peace.

The health benefits to my family have been amazing. When we do eat outside food usually because of social obligations, we can tell instantly if the food has chemicals and preservatives as we will get an immediate reaction: usually a slight headache or upset stomach.

What's Wrong With Healthy Takeout Food?

First, takeout food is just not as healthy as freshly prepared food. The bottom line is that food from outside comes from a business. The proprietor's goal is to make money. It's necessary to add ingredients to make the food tastier; therefore, you can count on extra salt, butter or butter flavor, oils and other perhaps artificial flavorings. Who wants to buy bland food?

Unless it's exorbitantly expensive, quality has to take a backseat to consideration of the bottom line, the profit. If the proprietor buys the absolute best quality, she has to pass the cost on to you. The cook will tweak the ingredients to find the best combination of taste and profit. Maybe he buys the best quality meat, but then for the sauce he may use artificial cheese.

Another point that is rarely considered is the mood of the cooking staff. If they are experiencing stress, anger or sadness, you can be sure that your food will be less tasty. It would be a stretch to say that the negative energy will "harm" you, but it certainly won't help.

Have you ever gone to your regular restaurant and ordered your favorite dish only to find that it was just a little off? Consider the mood of the cook.

Friends that we know were under considerable stress for financial and personal reasons. During this period when they cooked, their food was less tasty and less satisfying. It was difficult to pinpoint exactly what was different, but it gave credence to the idea that when a person cooks with love and high spirits, her food is so delicious.

How Do We Cook If We Don't Know How?

We start small. We boil things. We broil things. We bake things. We make simple food such as taking a chicken breast, rubbing it with olive oil and sprinkling salt and pepper on it. We broil or bake it.

We make salads. We make healthy sandwiches and wraps. We make oatmeal. We steam vegetables. We eat whole grain pasta.

Many people say they are too busy to cook. This too often is true, but we should never be too busy for our health. We can throw something in a slow cooker, add onions, a little garlic, vegetables and potatoes, a little tomato paste, seasonings, and a flavorful stew will be awaiting us. Today, you can just go on YouTube or Google what you wish to make, and all sorts of recipes and cooking tutorials will pop up. Maybe we cook only once or twice a week in the beginning.

You could prep meals for the week on the weekend by chopping up vegetables, making a sauce or salad dressing, and/or precooking some items. For example, you could roast a chicken and shred the meat for other quick meals. It requires some planning and organization but the results are tremendous. The key is to make the little changes as often as you can until you are making daily healthy choices.

Water Intake

Do you drink enough water a day? Do you have easy bowel movements daily? Is your urine a light straw color? If not, increase your intake. Sometimes headaches and joint pain are caused by dehydration. Reach for water instead of soft drinks or prepared juices which often have added sugar and corn syrup. Juices from the juicer and blender are very good for you as there are no artificial ingredients.

Exercise

We all know why we have to exercise. One problem is finding an exercise and sticking to it, making it part of our regular routine. How many times have we joined a gym, taken a class, bought sporting equipment and attire, starting out enthusiastic only to drop out after a few weeks?

We have to rethink exercise. How do we start to incorporate exercise into our lives so that it as routine as brushing our teeth?

We start very small. Walking is a good place to start. Walk up and down your driveway or the length of one block. Do only what your body can do. Do a little daily.

Find ways to add more walking into your daily schedule.

For example, you can park your car seven minutes away from your place of work. Your daily walk to and from work will be 14 extra minutes added to your daily routine. If you think about it, that's an extra 70 minutes or an hour and ten minutes per week; 280 minutes per month or four hours and 40 minutes which at about 20 minutes per mile is 14 miles monthly and 168 miles per year! Why not park a little further away every time you go someplace? Or take the bus or train past your stop and walk back. As you can see, a little effort adds up to big results.

In addition, do some stretching or calisthenic type of exercise. Start at five minutes for three exercises. For example, you can stretch your sides and arms, do five sit ups, three push ups and one yoga pose. We develop our routines by starting very small, something that we can consistently do. It is not reasonable to say, "I am going to exercise for 30 minutes every day if you never exercise. Repeat: Start very small, stay consistent and you will succeed. Just be patient and realistic. It took a while, in some cases a lifetime, to get out of shape, so it will take some time to get to a healthy fitness level.

On YouTube, you can find seven-minute workouts that are easy to do. Dr. Oz has his own seven-minute workout, but it is not for beginners. If seven minutes is too long, do five minute workouts or rest during the seven-minute ones. Add a five-minute walk. You can adapt and adjust as you wish. Just commit to doing a little.

When you feel ready, that is when you add on the exercises, add on the minutes to your walking. Perhaps after a month, six weeks or whatever works for you, you begin to think about joining a gym, going to the pool, playing a sport, or whatever interests you.

Take your time and only take this next step if you know you can be consistent.

Breathing

What about your breathing? Are you running around breathing from the top of your lungs? Take time to breathe with focus throughout your day. For example, when you are in line at the supermarket, you can do some of the breathing exercises you learned in the meditation chapter. You can do deep breathing in the car, on the bus or in front of the TV. You can do breathing exercises anywhere.

Relaxation

How do you unwind? Do you stare at the TV and play with technology for hours? Are you relaxing with food, alcohol, sex and/or drugs? Learn to relax another way. You could massage your feet, listen to music or spend time doing whatever activity relaxes you whether it is tinkering with your car or knitting a sweater. Whatever you choose to do, actually make time for it and do it as often as possible. It takes a long time to change a habit, but the only way to change it is to actually do a new behavior.

Meditation

By now you understand the priceless benefits of meditation, so honor your one minute daily. In addition, try to fit in your meditation pit stops throughout your day.

Your Thoughts

We have been working on creating good thoughts and throwing out harmful ones. In addition, we learn that so many times, people do not mean the things they say or do on a very deep level. People talk casually as we all do, and many times our actions are spontaneous without careful thought. We must not take things personally and make them bigger than they really are. Once we can look at situations and people in this manner, we may see things much clearer and things may not bother us.

If something really upsets you, then meditate on it. When you can literally breathe into it, you can make it actually diminish in importance, clearing your mind. Also, talk about it openly with either the person or someone else. Again, by speaking about your problem, the "importance" of the matter immediately shrinks.

Lastly, try to think the way Buddha thought:

Happiness does not depend on what you have or who you are.

It solely relies on what you think.

Beware of Rigidity in the Daily Routine

We see it all the time. People suddenly adopt a healthy routine and then they become so regimented that they feel compelled to exercise every day for a set amount of time. Or they begin eating really well and at a birthday occasion, they cannot even eat a sliver of cake. They won't take a sip of wine or have a cup of coffee that's not decaffeinated. They can only eat organic produce. They're invited to a gathering and bring their own food. They never eat certain foods even if they desire them.

Following a healthy routine is wise but rigidity is not. We are in this life, living in this moment. Sometimes a special occasion or another person's feelings are more important than remaining on our healthy routine. It's knowing when to stay on course and when to bend like the bamboo. Suggestion: Maintain a healthy regimen 80% of the time and save that 20% for the special times, holidays and unexpected moments in your life.

There are vegetarians and vegans who watch their consumption, yet on special occasions or on vacations, they might partake in the local fare, enjoying the famous cheese or fish dish for example. That is the charm of a well-lived life, seizing moments and living well.

A Healthy Daily Routine is Forever

Sometimes a person has a healthy routine and because she is feeling great, she might stop doing all the wonderful things because she feels she doesn't have to anymore. Healthy living doesn't stop because now you feel well. It is a lifetime commitment, and it should be as deeply ingrained in you as drinking water, brushing your teeth and filing your taxes. Be vigilant that you do not stop once you start feeling your best.

This is the way you now live.

CHAPTER SEVEN:
Our Relationships, The Animal Kind, Too

By now, we have worked on ourselves by having taken inventory of who we are and have made conscious changes to recognize and see our true selves. As we understand ourselves better, we can realize our strengths and deficiencies, making an effort to improve and become our very best selves. It is all within our reach.

To have better relationships, we must always work on ourselves. How can we become our healthiest in mind, body and spirit? What are the things we must do? What are the things we must or must not think? We are the ones in charge, the ones who have full control over ourselves.

When we bring negative emotions—jealousy, spitefulness, competitiveness, for example — to our relationships, it is because we are not emotionally balanced. If we have these feelings, we have to work on ourselves to be secure and grounded. How do we do this? We can do Reiki on our chakras to strengthen and heal them. Meditation and other healing modalities are all helpful. More importantly, we can make sure that we are living how we are supposed to be living. When we are content and on track, these emotions will not surface.

However, even if these negative emotions arise, we don't have to act upon them. We can still behave graciously and with compassion for ourselves as we are only human. By behaving well, that feeling will dissipate.

Problems in Relationships

We all desire connections, especially in our romantic relationships, where the other person "sees" and "understands" us. We all want recognition for who we are, and we long for the profound meaning that relationships can bring to our lives.

These high expectations can create disharmony. Many of the expectations have been influenced by social media, TV, film and books. We desire that "perfect" relationship which we have seen and observed.

It rarely exists.

Other expectations come from our family dynamic and social influences, but we have to recognize that our partner comes from another family dynamic.

Ironically, often the dynamics that were not predominant in our families are exactly the ones that we seek out because of our lack, curiosity or desire. Initially, the opposite is very desirable and then after a period of time, usually after the initial glow of romance dies, that very thing will annoy us. It will start to feel foreign and unfamiliar, and then we start wishing for our person to be different, to change to how we are. We forget how we once prized that characteristic, that style, or behavior.

What we have to remember is that we are all human and deeply connected. We must search for the best in the other person and appreciate those superior characteristics. This is easier said than done especially for those people in long relationships. We tend to be less tolerant and accepting of others' behaviors because through time, these differences become more pronounced and thus irritating to us.

If a relationship for the long term is desired, it's best to not put your loved one under the microscope. Don't overanalyze and pick your partner apart. Go back to the gratitude exercise and imagine your life without that person. Really appreciate who you are and look at yourself first before you cast a critical eye in the direction of a significant other. This is a major rule for any relationship.

When you find yourself critical, look at yourself first and ask the hard questions such as the following.

Am I bored with myself?

What am I not doing that I should be doing?

How am I developing myself?

How can I make my life better?

What is my role in my dissatisfaction?

Always remember to look at yourself. When you look at others, focus on their good points, and how this person has helped you to have a happy life. Don't forget all that this person has given and sacrificed for you.

Long-term relationships are built on finding the joy in each other. First and foremost, you must find your own personal joy. Without that, you will never be truly happy with anyone, and you will always be dissatisfied with your partner and yourself.

Life Is Not a Theme Park

Life is just not thrilling all the time; it is not reality TV which is a fantasy-staged world. Most of life is made up of routines, trying times interspersed wth special moments that make life worth living. These highlights and feel-good times are the glue that cement relationships together, and their importance is very precious.

Sometimes life is rough for a period of time, and we must accept and understand that bad times are not forever just as happy times are not forever. We can do our very best to smooth out the rough edges and get back on course whenever we are knocked off our paths. Acceptance plays a vital role in how successful we manage life. If we can accept what is, change what we can, and not dwell in negativity, then we have a very good chance of living an excellent life.

All relationships can benefit from Reiki but rather than putting the focus on your partner, Reiki yourself. When you are balanced, your thinking, your decision-making, your living will all be based on a clear, logical yet heart-based thought process. As a result, your relationships will flourish.

If you desire a relationship or friendship for the long haul, then sometimes take your foot off the gas and allow yourself to coast sometimes, seeing where it goes. And remember:

Be easy in your relationships.

Understand that no one understands you as well as you do.

No one can read your mind.

Most people do not intentionally try to hurt you.

People are as complex as you are, so be patient.

Sometimes allow your relationship to meander and go where it will, to just be.

If your person is of good character, then count yourself fortunate and hang on with appreciation.

Difficult People

There will always be problem people in our lives whether it's a parent, a relative, a neighbor, a boss, a cashier at the market. These people are all in pain. They either feel bad from physical health problems or they have suffered emotional hurts that have not been resolved. The kinder, the more generous, the more thoughtful a person is, indicates how happy and satisfied that person truly is. That said, one must deal with difficult people. What do we do?

Don't Forget Reiki Principle: Compassion

Treat difficult people with compassion first. When we can see another's point of view and imagine living and walking in his footsteps, then we can be a little easier and more accepting. When we react with compassion, the other person feels seen and that may be enough for the person to stop her prickly behavior. It can be that simple.

In one of my classes, I met Kathleen Croghan, a woman in her 90s who had been meditating for over 25 years and credits meditation for bringing her peace and deep compassion. She doesn't view people as difficult because she says that she feels a oneness with everyone, even criminals. She said, "Perhaps, if I had been raised in horrific circumstances, I might have made those bad decisions. I know that we are all the same, and I feel that I can connect with everyone."

Perhaps, we are not yet at the place where Kathleen is, so if we have tried patience and compassion and still we are having difficulties, then we must show confidence, firmness and the fact "that we have seen them." We let them know that we know exactly what they are about. We are not going to harangue them, nor will we allow them to walk all over us. When difficult people are put on notice, they act better. When difficult people see they are dealing with a person who responds back right away with strength and confidence, they attack less. Difficult people are at their absolute worst if they see people who are weak, insecure and unable to speak up. They will bully this person relentlessly.

Sometimes, we have to step away from people who repeatedly are cruel and insensitive even if they are family members. We always give our people chances, but if there is no resolution, then walk away from the abuse and make clear boundaries.

You cannot give Reiki to the difficult person, but you can Reiki yourself so you are at your most balanced. You also can Reiki the situation because you own a part of it. Usually people in Reiki II have this ability because they can also do long distance Reiki. Nevertheless, write down the situation on a piece of paper and hold it as you send Reiki to it.

Teach your children to stand up for themselves, a very vital and important lesson in today's world. Explain to them that they must never be the victim and to never tolerate rude or cruel behavior. They must not be mean or belligerent in retaliation, but they must be able to defend themselves with the right words and with conviction.

Show role-playing, so they will have effective retorts at their disposal. It's always better to answer back with humor because that technique confuses a bully. Always tell them to use their biggest voice, the one that comes from the stomach. Here are examples you can practice with a child (or even yourself!! Just adapt the correct age-appropriate dialogue).

What do you say if a kid says you're ugly?

You say, you need glasses.

What do you say if a kid says you're stupid.

You say, you're the one who's stupid because you can't recognize genius.

It's really not so important what you say although a witty, well-thought out retort is powerful, but that you answer back instantly. Many times, we are too surprised or stunned to reply, and then the bully "wins." By role-playing, by having an arsenal of words at your disposal, you are ready, and you will not be bothered again.

If your child can't think of anything quickly, they can always say in a loud voice:

Hey!   or   **Good!**

When my daughter was in the second grade, a classmate taunted her by saying that she had a mustache. My daughter, very proud of her half Persian heritage which gave her beautiful brows and an abundance of hair, shot back, "Too bad you're not Persian!" Needless to say, her would-be bully was totally speechless and never bothered her again.

Animals

Our pets are part of our families, and they love us unconditionally. When we have sadness, deep anger, resentment, worry and other negative feelings raging through us, our animals pick up on our feelings. Many will sacrifice themselves for our well-being by getting sick for us.

When a pet is very sick, look at the owners. Are they emotionally well? Are they harboring negative feelings? How are they living?

Obviously pets cannot speak, but if you look closely at them, they are speaking but in their own way. They may jump up and down at the prospect of a walk, chew things with nervous energy, refuse to meet your eyes, and so forth. They are speaking all the time, and it is up to us to notice how and what they are communicating.

Cats say a lot with their tails. Tails perfectly straight with the end curved like an upside down J indicates that all is well. When a cat swishes its tail back and forth, there is a general feeling of unease. Ears pricked back? Irritated. When their eyes close and they open to see you and then close again, they are showing their love.

A Daily Routine is Not Just For Humans

Animals, like ourselves, thrive on a strong daily routine. They need healthy food, regular exercise, time for play and time for relaxation and regular affection. They don't want to spend days and nights all by themselves. Neglect equals loneliness equals depression.

When owners are very busy and stressed out, it's very easy to neglect pets. Owners think *Oh, I'll skip Bailey's walk tonight. He won't mind.* On the contrary, Bailey minds a lot, but he will lie by his owner's feet as his owner plows through video games. Too many missed walks will create a lethargic Bailey, a dog with pent-up energy which one day will skyrocket into some type of destructive behavior, depression or illness. If we are depressed, then the energy in the home is low. If we harbor anger, then our home environment is fully charged with this negative emotion. Our animals will pick up on the energy and will be affected by it. This is how disease can begin in our pets.

Animals are our family members and when we choose to bring them home, we must honor that responsibility for the duration of our pets' lives by taking the best care of ourselves so that we can take the best care of them and create the most stable and loving environment.

In one situation, a couple was having marital problems that were unresolved. The husband went away on a business trip and the wife and their two dogs remained at home. During the week that he was gone, there was no conflict and the home environment was peaceful. As soon as the husband returned, the unresolved conflict came back to the forefront and the dogs got into a vicious fight and had to be separated.

This couple eventually divorced, and the wife took both dogs. One of the dogs had a skin condition and was showing signs of age. In the new home, within two weeks, the dog's coat became glossy and healthy, and the dog surprised his owner by jumping excitedly over a fence, something the owner thought not possible given his advanced age. Now the dog is showing no signs of aging or skin problems because the source of the anger is no longer present.

Thirteen years ago, my husband and I were deeply angry at each other. We could not reach a resolution, so we gave each other the silent treatment. Our home atmosphere was tense and heavy. This was the time that our cat got hit by a car. To us, this was no accident. When there is such a negative emotion in the environment, it has to act out somewhere and the poor recipient was our kitty. Fortunately, Lilybug healed, and my husband and I learned a valuable lesson.

The Hardest Thing

Being authentic can be the most difficult thing to be and to live on a consistent basis. Why? You would think being yourself is the most natural thing. It should be. Look at any child.

The problem is that society, ourselves, our circle of people and the media may put pressure on us—consciously or unconsciously—to behave, to think and to act a certain way. We don't want to be different because deep inside there is a fierce longing to belong, to fit in. No one wants to stand out for being outside the norm except famous people known for their talent, their craft, or even their infamy. They are the only ones who are given more rein to express themselves in their behavior, lifestyle, clothing and even their words, and they are usually celebrated for it. They can be weird or odd because their deeds, antics, wealth and fame are viewed as special; society puts them on a pedestal.

For most of us who are living regular ordinary lives, being different is difficult because we will stick out. However, if we are authentic to ourselves and comfortable with it, then others become at ease as well although initially they may tease or take jabs at us. If people see that you are secure and comfortable with yourself, then they accept you.

Being authentic is living your life how you normally live it when no one is looking. It is about accepting yourself the way you are and actually reveling in it. Our idiosyncrasies, our differences, our unique ideas all make us special.

When we are authentic, there is a natural ease because you don't have to think about what you are going to say or what you are going to do. You eliminate that stress by just being who you are. You just live.

Try to do things that you really want to do.

Surround yourself with people who really support you.

Say things that you truly believe in.

Just be who you really are.

Whenever I find myself trying to be whom I am not, that is usually when I'm steered in the wrong direction. If I listen to myself and try to act honestly, then life is just easier and smoother. One example would be when I worked in fashion in New York City. I was two years out of college, and I got hired by the premiere fashion magazine at that time. I remember going home to Los Angeles for Christmas and having one of my friends proudly introduce me to one of her friends with the descriptive line that I worked at… I remember feeling amazed by my friend's attitude.

I thought about my work and how it wasn't that meaningful for me. The magazine was a beautiful fantasy, and although I had always loved going through its pages, I knew that my true self was not anyone that was impressive or respected by my editors and fellow colleagues. They valued beauty, wealth, and prestige and my editor admired one's ability to craft a catchy headline instantly, all of which I was sorely lacking or could not do at that time.

Within six months, understanding that I had no future there, I went to human resources and asked if they could transfer me to any of their other magazines. It took a while and then I was at another magazine for younger women. It was better, but I knew that it, too, was not right for me and that this was not my path.

Later, when I moved back to Southern California, I found my way into teaching adult school and that was my truth. It wasn't glamorous or highly respected, but on a day-to-day basis, it was thoroughly satisfying. I loved teaching the students and I saw how my efforts impacted their lives in small ways as they progressed and reached their goals. I was happy because I was working authentically.

Last Words

There is a lot of information on these pages, and there are a lot of new habits, skills, and ideas to absorb. Look at everything as a small but ongoing process and you will be on your way. Break it down into steps and do what you can.

Everything and anything is achievable if it's done slowly, with intention and with realistic expectations.

Life is an adventurous process and yes, it's also hard work. But it's how you look at it.

I choose to see life as this exciting challenge and that I can be the recipient of all things good and wonderful. I have to work to get them, but I know I have the tools as we all do. It's just understanding that first I have to be as balanced and as healthy as possible, and then I can take the steps to achieve my goals.

I am also always reviewing my life, comparing how it is now to years ago, five years past, a year ago, six months ago, three months prior, last month, last week, yesterday. I always see results—big and small— and that always encourages me and gives me the heart to continue forward.

The secret is to live your own life, not to watch or copy others.

Don't be the person who's watching TV and movies all the time, on the computer, on your phone or pad every single night. These people miss the boat, and soon years have gone by and they have done nothing. They live their lives, but are not particularly happy. They believe that this is their only reality. They feel stuck.

No one is really stuck if they do not want to be. To get unstuck, you have to do the work. There is no quick fix, no magic, just the hard work. Do your work with gratefulness and joy.

Do self-Reiki regularly. It will help balance you and help you to acquire the new skills and habits that are literally life transforming. Do everything slowly and with intention. Reiki will give you the insight, the courage, and the stamina to endure. And you will find true joy.

Acknowledgements

In life, we come across so many different, special and even difficult people, who just by their mere presence can inspire, change or challenge us. For all those people that I have met in this journey of life, a sincere thank you.

A special thank you to Karen Mayeda who wasn't able to get through the first manuscript, which in itself, was valuable information. It helped me to clarify, to reorganize and to make the book more reader-friendly.

A heartfelt thank you to my readers, Barbara Hughes and Stanley Tahara for their insights and careful eyes.

Mari Fukuyama, my esteemed editor, and Bita Masoumi, my creative designer, get kudos for skillful editing and fine eyes which honed my manuscript into a real book. Thank you very much Mari! Thank you very much Bita!

Warm gratitude to my Reiki Master Teachers: Tuesday May Thomas (Levels I, II and III) and to Lauren Adamczyk (Reiki Master Teacher).

Always thank you to George Tahara for being a good father and for his open mind to test out my ideas and theories, for Hanna whom I have had the pleasure of parenting which has taught me so much, and for Lilybug, a most valued Reiki recipient.

All the thanks in the world to Sumiko Tahara for her honesty, her honor and originality. You never knew it, Mom, but you made all the difference in the quality of my life.

And most of all, thank you to Abbas who because of who he is and what he has done, has helped me to live my life the way I wish, which has been my greatest freedom, my most treasured gift.

Made in the USA
San Bernardino, CA
16 November 2018